10s & Xs

BY GARET L. GARRETT

BECOMING A COMPETITIVE SHOOTER AND
THE NUANCES OF COMPETITIVE SHOOTING

BOOKLOGIX®
Alpharetta, Georgia

ISBN: 978-1-61005-264-1

Library of Congress Control Number: 2012917631

Printed in the United States of America

This paper meets the requirements of ANSI/NISO Z39.48-1992
(Permanence of Paper)

Dedication

This book is dedicated to James L. McPeak, my English composition instructor at North Central Michigan College in Petoskey, Michigan, during the fall semester of 1962.

To you James...your dedication to your craft has not been wasted and is most humbly appreciated. Thank you.

Table of Contents

Acknowledgments

Posthumously, to my father, Glenn D. Garrett an unredeemable debt of gratitude for instilling within his children a familiarization of firearms handling, shooting, hunting, and the care and sportsmanship that goes with gun sports.

A sincere thank you to Dr. Judy Tant, seven time Women's National Pistol Champion at Camp Perry, Ohio, for her previewing *10s & Xs* and graciously offering her advice and expertise on more than a few relevant points.

A heartfelt thank you to close friend and competitor, Rolf V. Henretty for his patience and insistence as my instructor in getting me started in competitive pistol shooting.

To David H. Rinald for his contribution in providing suggestions for comfortable reading and continuity through his proofreading.

To Jorge A. Naranjo, my stepson, a very special note of gratitude. Without his invaluable contributions to this endeavor in design and layout this booklet would not exist.

And, to all of you out there with whom I shot shoulder to shoulder over the years, I offer you a similar thank you. From each of you I picked up bits of information that have helped me, and continue to help make my competitive and non-competitive shooting experiences a pleasure.

Introduction

"They can because they think they can."

– Publius Vergilius Maro 70 – 19 B.C.

My main purpose for writing this is to shed some light on some of the nuances of gun handling for the newer competitive shooters out there who wish to improve their skills. What I have compiled here are tips and information that hopefully will make the sport more fun for them and keep it fun for a lifetime. In so doing, I also hope to make a positive contribution to their successful transition and to make their journey a quicker one. The positive and productive qualities of shooting that I've observed, been taught, discovered on my own, and what comes naturally, are the things I wish to pass along to you, the reader.

This information is presented for shooters wanting to shoot one-handed, and primarily for the shooter entering the competitive arena. However, with few exceptions, everything herein applies to all shooters of pistols trying to hit a specific spot on a paper target. Throughout this text, I am writing from the perspective of a right-handed shooter using open sights.

I feel that shooters having the greatest distance to go to achieve expert status, will benefit the most by reading this booklet. Those of you who aren't fortunate enough to have the one-on-one coaching that I had, will also benefit greatly if you apply yourself.

Since guns have always been a big part of my heritage and my growing up, I wish to pass along a special and silent "Thank You" to my father Glenn D. Garrett for his lifetime of encouragement in the shooting sports, and to my three brothers, Jack, Pete, and Pat. We shot alongside each other in the field and between the trap-houses through those many memorable years.

With the able assistance (and unlimited patience) and the one-on-one coaching of Sfc. Rolf V. Henretty with the pistols of all calibers, and Lt. Col. Norman Goelzer with the match grade M-14 service rifle, I have discovered the joys of competitive shooting without making work out of it. Did I have to work at it? Oh, yes! Should working at it be laborious or painful? Never, and it never has been.
To these fine individuals and a hundred other appreciated weekend, evening and Sunday shooters who have made a positive contribution to my shooting skills, such as they are, I would like to extend my heartfelt thanks for my continuing interest in the fraternity of competitive shooting sports.

George Bernard Shaw once said, "Those that can, do. Those that can't, teach." Right here let me confess to not being a champion class shooter in any of the shooting sports many disciplines. In all of my sixty-plus years of shooting (since the age of ten) I never

achieved an expert class rating with a pistol of any caliber, indoors or out, nor have I gone higher than a marksman class rating with any rifle, indoors or out. Though I have shot "25 Straight" three times in skeet with a model twelve 20 gauge, I shot them all at least forty years ago, and none of them in registered competition. My main interest now is in schuetzen rifles and schuetzen competition.* While I love all types of shooting, I feel that the schuetzen game is truly the gentleman's shooting sport, and one that will severely test the man, his ego, and his equipment to the fullest.

What follows is a series of short chapters presented in the order that I think is the most appropriate and will be the most helpful to a new pistol shooter. However, 99 percent of it also applies to rifle shooters.

From this point on, there will be one overriding factor in every facet of your shooting, and that is COMFORT, mental and physical COMFORT. Because of my strong feelings for its importance in shooting, I have capitalized the word and its variables throughout this text to the point that you will probably get sick of looking at it, and partially that's the whole point of doing it. Until you consistently shoot COMFORTABLY, or as COMFORTABLY as conditions will allow, you will not shoot your capable best.

Notes

Chapter One
Pistol Selection

Go to a range with shooting friends and try the guns that they shoot. Before you go to the gun shop, you should have a reasonably good idea what gun you want and what's appropriate for the kind of shooting you intend to do.

Ask the shooters lots of questions about the type of shooting you are interested in. They have probably been down the road you're about to travel, and they may make your trip a lot easier, faster, and maybe cheaper.

Selecting a handgun at the dealer's showroom is NEVER a matter of looking in the showcase and saying, "Boy, that one sure looks nice. I'll take that one." A proper selection demands that you find a gun that will allow you to shoot it accurately with the least amount of effort. It needs to fit your hand (as well as your head) and be as COMFORTABLE in your hand as it can be. Its weight and balance must already be one of the acceptable features of the gun, not a feature you'll "take care of later." The recoil that the gun will produce must also be an important consideration.

Try several pistols for proper grip size, heft, balance, sight features for adjustability, and above all else, your ability to see a sharp and clear definition of and distinction from both the front and rear sights while the gun is extended in your hand in a "reasonably proper" shooting stance. To some people the color of the gun is a factor of choice, one that should be on the bottom of your list of feature priorities. The best contrast for the best sight picture is soot-blackened sights silhouetted against a white paper target. Neon pink, or green, or shiny chrome sights will not even be close to efficient in competitive bull's-eye shooting, and no one has ever been awarded extra points just for having a pretty gun.

Your fingers should wrap COMFORTABLY around the pistol grips to the point that their tips are nearly pointing straight back at you. If your fingertips are pointing more to the left than back, the grip is probably too large for you. Conversely, if it feels like you're gripping a skinny broom handle; the grip is too small to be competitively effective. Either condition will defeat your ability to control the recoil and consistently hit the bull's-eye. If you have to think about how you're gripping your gun while you're shooting, your scores will suffer every time.

The grips of competition pistols are replaceable and are about the only thing that can be readily changed to affect COMFORT. There are a great variety of grips available on the market. However, there are very few, if any, that will make the original grips smaller.

Other factors to consider are the design characteristics of the gun. If any of them detract in the slightest way from what feels COMFORTABLE to you, try other models, other makes, or even another caliber. If the size of the holes you will put in the target is not really important to you, at the very least the placement of the holes in the target should be. It is possible to select a gun that will not allow you to achieve the degree of acceptable or superior marksmanship you desire. Always remember, it's fit and COMFORT first.

Keep in mind when making your gun selection, that if you labor to shoot it with any degree of consistent accuracy you will not enjoy the sport as much, and subsequently, you will not want to shoot as often as you might otherwise. You may even give up shooting altogether because it isn't as much fun as you thought it would be, and shooting really is great fun when you do it correctly with the correct equipment.

A master class shooter can probably pick up any pistol and shoot it as well as it will allow them to, but in serious competition they will not shoot just any gun. They will only shoot what is absolutely right for them. Let's face it: they didn't achieve master class status by shooting good scores with guns that were just so-so or wrong for them.

One of the great fallacies about finely tuned and very light trigger pulls, compared to heavy trigger pulls, is the lighter the pull the better. An extremely crisp and light trigger is ideal in the hands of a very experienced and good shooter. On the other hand, a heavy trigger pull will force a new shooter to concentrate more on front sight alignment while exerting that greater degree of pull force on the trigger. A better shooter will emerge over time if they start out with a heavy trigger pull and "graduate" to a lighter trigger pull.

Whether or not you can shoot a very light trigger, the NRA rules are very specific about how light a trigger pull can be in sanctioned competition. The rule has nothing to do with your ability to shoot a light trigger. It's a safety factor, first and foremost. You should have a rule book anyway, so check it for the correct trigger pull on your pistols.

A very good friend of mine, and a very good rifle shooter, in past years, used to keep an excessively heavy pull trigger assembly handy for those few occasions when he "strayed" from holding sight alignment as steadily as he should have with his tuned triggered competition rifle. When that happened to him during a match, he simply exchanged assemblies and continued the match, only now he's using a tutorial reminder, forcing him to put his concentration where it belonged—on the front sight. A heavier than normal trigger pull on your pistol can be (is) a good training tool, whether it's used by the new shooter in practice, or as an occasional re-educating tool for the experienced shooter. Good shooters are continually reminding themselves of this basic principle of shooting.

Chapter Two
The Grip

When a competitive shooter places the gun in their shooting hand, they do so by using the non-shooting hand to push, or seat, the gun into the shooting hand to facilitate its proper gripping position. You are leaving yourself at a disadvantage if you simply pick up your gun with your shooting hand and proceed to use your fingers as if you're wadding up a piece of paper to find your best grip. Use your non-shooting hand to grasp the barrel and PUT, PLACE, SEAT, FORCE the gun in your shooting hand for your best and proper grip, don't just pick it up with your shooting hand like you're going to casually examine it.

Shooters preparing their targets for a match

For a person with five fingers with which to grip the gun, only three are necessary: the thumb, the middle finger and the ring finger. The pinky, or the little finger, should contact the pistol grip but it doesn't need to do anywhere near the gripping job that the other three do. In essence, the little finger contacting the gun is incidental. A firm but non-working contact by it will suffice, if the caliber and the pistol size can be correctly handled.

The thumb should have gripping contact pressure at least to the first knuckle. From there to the tip it can stick out into the air. When the pad of the thumb and the little finger are used to hard grip a gun there is a tendency to "milk" the grip and cause you to work harder than is necessary to maintain sight alignment. When they're "working" they tend to do what is referred to as "helping the shot" and can cause shots to be "pushed or pulled" and to strike the target somewhere other than the bull's-eye.

When I give one-on-one advice to shooters, I tell them that I think of a shooter as being divided into two parts. Part one is the entire body (with the exception of the trigger finger) and all its parts. All those body parts have only one job, and that job is to do whatever is necessary to correctly align and maintain the alignment of the front sight and the rear sight to each other while the target sits as quietly atop the front sight (blade) as you can hold it. Part two is the trigger finger all by itself. And its only purpose is to move the trigger rearward without disturbing what part one has accomplished (that good sight picture) until the gun fires. For the trigger finger to do its job correctly it must be correctly, placed on the trigger. Part of selecting the "right" gun is being able to place your gripping fingers around the grip and your trigger finger correctly on the trigger, with everything else also being right.

If you had someone gently nudge the muzzle of your pistol to the left or right as you were shooting, the bullet would go to the left or the right, and it would be more difficult for you to maintain sight/target alignment. If your finger is placed incorrectly on the trigger that's exactly what is happening, and the results should be predictable. It may seem like a very small left or right movement at the muzzle, but at the target where the results show up, the holes can be a few, or many, inches left or right of the bull's-eye. That can translate to more than a few points that you've lost just from the improper placement of your finger. When you add that condition to all the other "almost perfect" conditions you may be accepting over the entire course of a match, they can add up to a considerable and unnecessary scoring deficit.

If you don't have your finger far enough in on the trigger you will tend to "push" the shot to the left because you are using the end of the bone in your finger to pull the trigger, not the side of the bone. Like everything else in nature, the trigger wants to take the path of least resistance, so it tries to sneak out around the unsupported fleshy tip of your finger. What the finger is doing is pushing the trigger to the left and pulling it to the rear at the same time, instead of just pulling straight rearward. In so doing, the gun muzzle moves to the left also, albeit ever-so-slightly.

Conversely, if you have your finger in on the trigger so far that the crease of the first joint overlaps the trigger you will tend to "pull" the shot and shoot to the right. The bending of the finger, which is actually an arcing motion, wants to draw the gun muzzle to the right ever-so-slightly, and you only need a few ever-so-slightlys during a match to ruin what should have otherwise been a fun day of shooting. If you don't realize that you're doing it, you won't know what to correct. Look at where you place your finger on the trigger when you grip the gun. If you have to compromise either proper trigger finger position or proper overall grip of the pistol for the appearance of being ready to shoot, you have the wrong gun in your hand.

The correct position for your finger on the trigger is to center the trigger on the fleshy part of the end of your finger, where the whorls of your fingerprint are, as closely as you can. What you are trying to achieve is the travel of the trigger straight rearward without forcing you to maintain your sight alignment picture. Being close to correct isn't good enough. Besides, it negates all the work the rest of your body went through to make the shot good. Don't make your trigger finger apologize to the rest of your body for an errant shot, or vice versa.

Some shooters carry a rosin bag, the kind baseball pitchers or bowlers use, in their shooting boxes to help ensure they have a dry, positive and secure non-slip grip on the gun. Indoors or out-of-doors, conditions are not always as ideal as we'd like them to be for good shooting. Nervousness and/or atmospheric conditions may cause you to have slightly moist hands, a condition that will not allow you to grip your gun with the degree of confidence or proficiency necessary for you to shoot well. A rosin bag and a clean cloth hand towel will help you overcome some of that concentration theft.

The amount of grip pressure that you apply to your gun should be sufficient for you to control the gun for initial sight alignment, allow the gun to function properly, and to counteract or minimize the recoil in preparing for the next shot. Any grip pressure you exert over or beyond those requirements is an energy thief and will, over the course of a 2700 match, be destructive to your goals.

A reactionary tighter grip at the instant of recoil, because of the recoil, is incorrect for two reasons, only one of which I will address now, and is worse than useless. Once you have had to do this, or think you need to do it, you have set yourself up to flinch on the next shots as well, and you will undoubtedly overcompensate with your grip for a while because your mind is now thinking about the recoil to come. By doing this, you've just divided your concentration, and divided concentration is the same as no concentration. At this point maybe you should consider the fact that you have more gun in your hands than you can presently handle.

The proper grip pressure should be COMFORTABLE, but almost so intense that it causes the gun to tremble, but not quite. To find out how that feels, hold the gun out in a sighting posture. Slowly increase your gripping pressure until the gun starts to tremble. Now relax your grip slowly until the gun becomes steady, or as steady as you can hold it. This is now the grip pressure you should be using. It's the best you can achieve for now. ACCEPT IT, for now. Grip exercises will help you strengthen your gripping ability and gripping endurance and make proper gripping much less tiring over the course of a complete 270 shot match.

It should be understood that there is a definite difference between a shooter-induced "tremble" and a shooter's normal "wobble" area. Your normal wobble area is the distance the front sight travels in any direction over the target when the gun is held correctly (as above) while you are aiming at the target. A normal wobble is generally a much slower motion than is a tremble. This is, of course, assuming that you are in reasonably good health and not under the influence of alcohol, coffee, tobacco, or other stimulants. In a wobble, the sights may be aligned to each other all the time you are aiming, they just simply won't stay stationary on the target. In a tremble, the sights are never aligned to each other or on the target long enough to rely on the shot going where it should.

A wobble area is generally reducible if you are dedicated to working at shooting properly, do grip exercises, are COMFORTABLE on the line and learn to relax intentionally. Taking a few deep breaths may help to relax your body a little, but it won't do a thing for your mind. The ability to relax your mind at will for the time length of a three-gun match takes time and requires a dedicated regimen of practice to work in harmony with a relaxed body.

Some people's hands shake badly in every facet of their lives and they appear to be nervous about everything. When such a condition is taken to the firing line, this "natural characteristic" produces their normal wobble area, and probably some tremor. If they were to grip the gun harder in an effort to reduce this condition they would induce even more muzzle motion that would make accurate shooting virtually impossible.

If you are in the slow fire stage of shooting at a match, or in practice, and things just aren't happening the way you want them to, place the butt of the gun down on the bench while maintaining a relaxed position grip. A proper position grip for a benched gun is just enough grip pressure to maintain the feeling that the pistol is still being correctly held, but not tiring the hand or the forearm.

While you're resting the bottom of the grip of the gun on the bench, ease up a little on your shooting grip, give your hand and arm a break and let them regain some of the strength needed to hold the gun correctly for the next shots. Reestablish as much of the COMFORT as you can with which you started. In slow fire, there is a lot of time to allow for this. Take advantage of every opportunity that gives you an edge. In a sanctioned pistol match, you have ten minutes to fire ten rounds in the slow-fire stage. If you are the last person to fire shot number ten, so what? If it takes you ten minutes to calm down, feel right, catch your breath, or wait for your heartburn to go away, take the ten minutes—they're yours. You're entitled to them. You're not trying to beat the clock or your neighbor. You're trying to shoot ten shots as accurately as you can in ten minutes, period.

Remember that the energy you spend unnecessarily early in the match may be reflected in your scores later. Target shooting is not a Herculean sport and it doesn't require bulging muscles, super strength, or a sports jock's body. The longer you are involved in any shooting the more you will realize that it is a sport of finesse. In fact, more finesse is required for shooting 10s and Xs at twenty-five and fifty yards than is required for success in any other sport. If you think you need a tighter controllable grip, you will need to develop an exercise regimen for your hands, arms, and shoulders to strengthen the muscles, and physical conditioning, for the whole body as well, will improve your scores.

When I started to shoot in competition for the military, I asked Sfc. Henretty, a Distinguished Expert pistol shooter, close friend, and shooting companion, "How much grip pressure should I apply to the army's .45 automatic while shooting ball ammunition?" His response was, "Grip it hard enough that you force a drop of gun oil to ooze out the bottom of the magazine slot, then let off just enough to draw the drop back up." That's obviously a trifle extreme, but I got the message.

On two separate occasions, one at an army match at Fort Riley, Kansas, and the other at the National Matches at Camp Perry, Ohio, I'm glad I followed his advice. The .45's that I was shooting, one my own and the other the army's, went fully automatic after the first shot of a five shot string, and with ball ammunition no less. In each case, the rapid discharge of the next four rounds happened so fast that if my grip had been on the light side, a reactionary recovery grip might have been too late. Under these conditions, the muzzle attitude change of a .45 automatic pistol is so quick and so great that if I hadn't had a correct grip to begin with people could have been hurt or killed. Only one full auto incident like that will make a believer out of anyone.

On the scary side, too light a grip on a loaded big bore semi-automatic with a grip safety, such as the 1911A1 .45 automatic has, can cause second and third discharges without your intent. What happens is, upon recoil the gun is forced backward into the fleshy webbing between your thumb and trigger finger. (Exactly where it should be to disengage the grip safety in order for you to fire it.) While this is going on, your trigger finger is still on the trigger making "incidental" contact, but now doing so with a moving gun. The three conditions needed to fire such a loaded gun have been met. But now your grip is loose, and what the gun can do now is of major concern.

What happened to me in both cases was caused by broken sears. There was no way that I know of to have prevented them. On the other hand, whether it's your guns or your support gear, frequently inspected and well maintained equipment will function longer, more reliably, more accurately and, most assuredly, safer. Good maintenance of yourself and your equipment is, and should be, part of the COMFORT zone in which you need to be. If your equipment is well maintained, you should be able to "reasonably" expect it to work properly, thereby allowing you to rely on it to perform as you wish, when you wish, part breakage aside.

There are probably more than a few other nasty horror stories floating around out there about light grips and .45 caliber semi-automatics. Concerning this possibility, the very fact that it is a large bore handgun in your hand should be tacit evidence and acknowledgement that you should heed the advice about a necessary proper grip.

When shooting "Automatic" pistols there are several items concerning the grip that pertain only to them. Because they are designed to function at their best when shot from a relatively unyielding platform—your arm, grip, and locked wrist—a firm grip is necessary for their proper functioning. I know first-hand that too light a grip on a .38 semi-automatic, shooting surface flush wad-cutters, can cause the bullets to tumble and go through the target sideways—key holing—in as short a distance as fifty feet.

Even with other semi-automatics, if you lessen your grip too much the slide action will become "spongy" and the slide may not fully cycle to effectively extract and/or eject spent cases from the ejection port. And, although the slide may appear to have returned to battery (full forward) and completed the cycling, the gun may not be cocked. Partial cycling of the slide may eject the spent cartridge but not pick up the next round from the clip, in which case there may not be a live round in the chamber even if the slide did return to battery.

Because of a less than firm grip you may also experience what is termed "smokestacking" or having the ejecting cartridge only partially clear the ejection port before the slide can complete its return to the battery position. This is a condition which occurs when the spent case is trapped by the forward moving bolt face and stands the cartridge vertically on end, or sideways, and looking very much like a small brass smokestack. When that happens, your shooting stops until you clear the spent cartridge. In some cases, you may be denied an alibi string of fire for clearing, or trying to clear, the smokestack. This will be discussed later in the booklet.

Smokestacking can happen for several reasons. Because of a loose grip, the bolt/slide didn't cycle rearward far enough to flip the spent cartridge clear of the ejection port before the slide tried to return to battery. This is called "short stroking." Another reason could be that either the extraction spur on the bolt face or the ejection pin alongside the bolt, or both, are worn, bent, or otherwise in disrepair. Such conditions can cause them to fail to grip the spent cartridge cleanly and apply enough flip motion to the cartridge to send it flying clear of the port before the slide returns to battery.

A clip that extends too high into the receiver, or has one, or both, cartridge retaining ears bent upward too far may impede the free motion of the slide because the bottom of the bolt/slide is rubbing on the ear(s) of the clip. This can result in a delaying action in the slide, rearward or forward, and will contribute to smokestacking, among other things. It may allow the slide to almost return to battery but not quite. The physical visual difference between a fully returned and an almost fully returned bolt can be so slight that you may wonder what the problem is because the crack between the bolt face and the chamber looks normal to you. It may not be. Check for shiny wear marks on the tips of your clip's ears and on the underside of the bolt if you have persistent slide return failure or smoke-staking problems.

If you do, this may be your problem. These are not, by any means, the only conditions that might cause loading, extraction, and ejection problems with semi-automatic pistols. If you have stainless steel gun parts or magazines, you may need to apply some machinist's bluing to the suspect surfaces to detect evidence of rubbing parts. All of the preceding is said on the assumption that you are shooting factory loads. If you are shooting reloaded ammunition, there is a completely different set of considerations that come into play.

Once you learn to rely on your equipment and trust it, you can dismiss any concerns about it from your proper focus and concentration. There are no good excuses for not maintaining your guns properly. If you're old enough to own them and/or mature enough to shoot them like a true sportsman, you're also old enough and mature enough to learn how to take care of them properly, and then do it, on a regular basis.

Notes

Chapter Three
Ammunition

First, if it's not the right cartridge, or you don't know for sure if it's the right cartridge for the gun, or if it's damaged or dirty, DON'T allow it to be put in yours or anyone else's gun. With one shot, one tiny grain of sand adhering to a bullet for whatever reason can instantly turn a great shooting gun into an expensive wall hanger. The more important message here is not the sand, but the issue of safety. Any one of the conditions mentioned is potentially very dangerous.

Second, if it's a reloaded round and you don't have trusting reassurances about the qualifications of the person that reloaded it, or don't know who reloaded it, DON'T allow that cartridge to be put in your gun, or a gun you're shooting. If you have any doubts or questions about what the proper ammunition is for your gun, consult a reputable gunsmith, dealer, or fellow club member whose advice is trusted and often sought.

There are many reputable "for pay" individuals out there to choose from that reload cartridges, and every organized club with any longevity has members that can steer you in the right direction to give you the correct help on the subject when needed. Consider these individuals as a part of your shooting toolbox, as a tool that you may not often use, but one you can rely on when needed. The important message that I'm trying to convey here is that if you have any degree of distrust in your ammunition, for whatever reason, don't even think about shooting it. It's a moot point to be angry with someone after the gun has exploded in your hand, ruining the gun and maybe you too.

If your shooting consists of just plinking, any ammunition that is correct for your gun and goes "BANG" may be adequate for you. However, to the serious competitive shooter intent on shooting only 10s and Xs, it should be known that all ammunition of one description is definitely not the same.

The ammunition that one manufacturer produces can be, and often is, markedly different operationally in your gun, and also with respect to accuracy, than what other manufacturers produce. If they weren't different, there wouldn't be any reason for choosing one brand over another except for the price. It's in the manufacturers' financial best interest to give us the "best" ammunition they can produce, and they all try to do just that. But, when the batch, or the material of a recipe or formula runs out they mix a new batch, and that's where the differences come in, even within a single manufacturer. Despite their best intentions, Lot #1234 can perform amazingly and decidedly different from "Lot #1234-With Supposedly Nothing Different" simply because there is something in their processes, or materials, or formulas that is not precisely repeated. In other words, there are differences from batch number to batch number.

The elements of difference between Lot #1234 and Lot #1234-WSND include the minute variables in the cartridges, the humidity level in the powder room or the assembly room, and the age of the priming compound or primers. There could be something in the case manufacturing processes, the powders formulae and their manufacturing processes, the bullets, and/or the whole cartridge assembly process with all its associated and mechanical variables. And if the truth were known, this might be the short list.

When any new materials or conditions are introduced into any process in order to be able to continue the manufacturing of the same product—any product—the end result will be different. New dies are replaced because of wear or breakage. Temperatures and atmospheric conditions, even in controlled-atmosphere rooms, fluctuate slightly. The speed of the assembling process may be altered slightly for whatever reason. When any of these things happen, there will be differences in the end product. There may be absolutely nothing even slightly amiss with the manufacturer's processes. It's just the nature of the business—all manufacturing—and the way it is. In the end the "new" product will look exactly the same and measure and weigh exactly the same as their "best" past product and it will function in your gun as well as any other ammo the company ever produced. But, despite all that sameness, it may not be as accurate as Lot #1234, in your gun. On the other hand, it might be amazingly more accurate. Staffs of highly qualified engineers are working hard to minimize and eliminate these variables so that all of the Lots they are producing are the good Lots, and will be in high demand by us. Let's face it, the "better" their ammo performs and the better your scores are because of it, the longer they stay in business and the more money they make.

Despite those good efforts, the different manufacturer's formulae and processes are still filled with variables. As a result, what may shoot well in John's gun may not shoot worth a hill of beans in your gun, or vice versa. Not only might a given brand not shoot accurately in your gun, if you're shooting a semi-automatic pistol it may not permit the gun to function correctly. It may not feed right, or it may not extract cleanly and efficiently. Other bug-a-boos might also enter the picture but that doesn't necessarily make it a bad Lot for everyone—maybe just for you.

Try different brands and Lot numbers of ammo to find out which perform most desirably (best) in your gun. At this point in the shooting game, you'll want to (should) start taking notes, copious notes. Write in your notebook which brand is best (so far) for a particular gun for what you're trying to accomplish. Include the Lot number(s) and the manufacturer and buy as much of the good stuff as you can afford (obeying all local, state and federal ordinances, of course). Ammunition is not going to get any cheaper, and you might as well shoot the stuff that makes you the happiest.

If you're planning to get into the reloading end of the shooting game, you should take precise notes on what it is you are doing. If you don't, you won't reach your goal of tight little groups of shots at fifty feet, twenty-five yards, or fifty yards very soon, if ever. Developing and ultimately finding what will perform best for you will be time-consuming and should always be a labor of love. But it is critically important that you understand the importance of the quality of the materials you use in your reloading process.

There are "better" powders, and "better" cases, and "better" bullets and primers for better accuracy. Those "better" ingredients, in the right combination, may work only for you. That's what you need to find out by going through the experimenting and winnowing process. What you use and the process by which you bring them all together is paramount to any degree of accuracy you will, or hope to, achieve with them. If you really want 10s and Xs, you will not settle for "close enough" in your reloading components or your reloading process.

As a precision shooter, if you're casting your own bullets, you have entered into a labor-intensive endeavor. You must weigh every bullet and carefully examine each of them for surface imperfections. For targets at the twenty-five yard range, all the bullets you shoot for record should be within two tenths of a grain of the same weight, i.e. 203.5 grs +- .2gr. That's not a difficult thing to accomplish if you're careful and consistent in your casting procedure. For fifty-yard targets I would accept only one weight, i.e. 203.5 gr + - .0 gr. The bases of each of the cast bullets must be perfect and unblemished. A nick or a rounded edge on the bullet's base will skew the bullet upon exit from the barrel when you shoot it, and tend to throw the shot off course. And, nobody wants skewed shots.

The greater the distance to the target, the more accurate your ammunition has to be. The gun isn't going to get more accurate from day to day if it's a good gun already, so the mechanical accuracy element of the equation has to come from your reloaded cartridges. When you're in charge of developing your own accurate loads, or getting rid of the subtle but troubling nuances in what you shoot, you are well into receiving a second self-fulfilling reward from the game of shooting, particularly when you succeed.

Start with one of the many excellent reloading manuals that are readily available, and rely on it. Any good gun shop will generally have a wide selection of reloading pamphlets to give away. They are supplied by the powder manufacturers to the dealers for people just like you. Pick up one of each for your new shooting library. Don't even try to remember what your recipes are. Look them up, either in your own notes or in the manufacturer's manuals. When you're getting ready to start a reloading session, place the open books within easy view and reach so you can refer to them often. The implications of the phrase, "Measure twice, cut once," are even more important here than in the carpenters or plumbers trades. There it just means the price of another board or pipe. Here it could mean adversely changing your health.

Working up "the" load for your particular gun should turn out to be only minutely different from what is in the books. By minutely, I mean tenths of a grain at a time. Any deviations that you make from the manual's recommendations should be very small and thoroughly discussed with an experienced and qualified reloader or gunsmith before you begin the process. If you are systematic and precise, demand good results and keep good records as your years of reloading experience accumulate, your new knowledge on the subject should gradually elevate you to the status of a qualified expert, also.

This is not a time for assumptions and macho attitudes. Know that you're headed in the right direction with your plans. Know that when you're shooting your reloads, the worst thing that will happen to you when you pull the trigger is that you might miss the bull's-eye. A bigger bang or a harder recoil does not equate to 10s and Xs. There is a "professionalism" here in the make-up of the serious competitive shooter that is also a necessary part of his mental toolbox that engenders a high degree of COMFORT.

Again, if there is even the slightest question in your mind about what you are doing or trying to accomplish, call a reputable gunsmith or someone in your club that has a proven record of accomplishment in reloading and talk to them about it. And keep asking your questions, because until you get the right answers, you are still as big a hazard to the shooter of your reloads as you were before you made the phone call(s). Check and double check, in writing, all the materials and measurements involved and make whatever notes you think will thoroughly cover the subject. Don't write notes that may be confusing the next time you look at them, which may be a year from when you penned them, but don't be afraid to write a lot of notes. You just may want to be physically able to come back and use an eraser on one of those notebook entries to improve upon your own recipe for success.

Notes

Chapter Four
Clothing

What you wear when you shoot may seem like a trivial matter. But, if what you wear is constricting, binds, or flops around in the wind, is too loose or is a distraction in any way, it will diminish your ability to perform at your best. On the other hand, you should wear anything that will allow you to shoot as well as you can, up to the point of being against the rules, or a distraction to the person next to you.

Your upper body clothing (sleeves in particular) must allow you to fully extend your arm with a minimum of effort under the present weather conditions. They must not be so heavy that they weigh adversely on your arm and cause you to think about the extra effort needed to support it and the gun for a minimum of twenty-two seconds. Again, we come back to the COMFORT factor.

There will be times when the weather dictates bulkier clothing, but even these clothes should not restrain your freedom of motion. Heavier clothing may even act as a motion dampener and tend to null your wobble area somewhat. The insulating properties of today's fabrics have pretty much reduced or eliminated any clothing weight problems. You may be shooting against someone who can tolerate cold weather to the point of wearing much less clothing than you. If so, if you are wearing a heavy jacket to be in your COMFORT zone, they may have a slight advantage over you over the course of the match.

Another aid to your shooting COMFORT is having a place to put your non-shooting hand while the shooting hand is doing its thing.

Trousers and pants, or culottes with pockets, will provide that place. With the non-shooting hand tucked away in the side pocket you can relax a little more, and by tucking your hand away you have reduced the amount of your body surface that the wind blows against as it flows around you. Some shooters slip their flattened non-shooting hand under their belts, some in the back, and some in the front. It's just a matter of preference.

The idea is to keep from having a loose sail hanging out there to catch any sudden breeze that comes along. If the wind is strong enough to move a loosely hanging arm, that movement is transmitted all the way to the gun. If any part of your body moves, the gun also moves, always. It's a movement that may be extremely slight and you may force the gun back on target without realizing it, but it does move.

To most people, standing with their hands in their pockets is part of a natural and COMFORTABLE posture, more so than standing with them just dangling down and loose. The same line of logic applies to the shooting stance. Like everything else in this game, strive for COMFORT. The warmth of your trousers, skirt, or upper body garb should also be appropriate for the weather and the demands of competing.

When shooting a .22 it might be prudent to wear a shirt that can be buttoned at the collar. A freshly extracted .22 cartridge from your neighbor's semi-automatic pistol is extremely hot, and it audibly sizzles when it lands on your bare skin, and especially so when it lands inside your unbuttoned shirt collar and is trapped against your neck. It leaves a burn mark outline of the hot case where it lands. In timed and rapid fire, when you don't have time to be putting out fires, sizzling skin puts a serious strain on your ability to maintain your concentration, and by the time you get it back to an acceptable level, your time may have run out, thereby forcing you to eat ten or twenty points. That one hot case may cost you the match. In slow fire, it still burns, but at least you have time to shake it out, reestablish your necessary level of COMFORT and concentration and get on with the match with minimal damage to your score and your pride.

If you do a lot of shoulder-to-shoulder competitive shooting around .22 semi-automatics, you will be "baptized by fire" eventually. So, since you're going to be wearing a shirt anyway, consider wearing one that you can button at the collar and minimize at least one more negative aspect of the game.

A reasonably stiff-brimmed hat or cap should also be a part of your wardrobe while you're trying to shoot 10s and Xs. It's a good way to help you stay warm, and, conversely, under a torrid sun, help keep you cooler. It will also keep your hair (if you still have any) from blowing around and possibly becoming a minor distraction.

Depending on the time of the day and where you must stand, it will give you some degree of relief from sunlight in your eyes or hitting your glasses and affecting your ability to see clearly. On a rainy or drizzly day (if you must) it may help to keep the water from going down the back of your neck and raising havoc with your concentration. Again, it's COMFORT.

Shoes should be COMFORTABLE and have as wide a sole surface contacting the ground, or floor, as you can get (no clown shoes, please). The reason for this is to give you the most stable shooting platform available. The ground where you're going to have to stand may not be perfectly level or smooth, so this is one external condition that you can control to some degree. Take advantage of it. If you're trying to maintain a desirable balance while wearing your favorite old, worn, and narrow soled sneakers, or heels, (cowboy boots) you are putting yourself at a measurable disadvantage right from the start. You need all the natural balance you can get to perform well and you shouldn't have to fight to get it while you're trying to concentrate on the front sight. Once the shooting starts, nobody cares what you look like. So, since you're not at a fashion show, lace-up work boots or oxford style lace-up shoes are perfect for providing the necessary stable shooting platform. Avoid any footwear that is loose or tight fitting and UNCOMFORTABLE.

Chapter Five
Safety Glasses

Along with wearing apparel, in the "automatically included" category, are SAFETY GLASSES. Whether you wear glasses to enable you to see or not, shatterproof safety glasses should be worn when you shoot, ALWAYS! Regular glass lenses should be augmented with a minimum of plastic safety glasses. Wearing only regular lenses while shooting is like thinking you paid the insurance bill last month as a tree is falling on your house. You don't have any protection. If you can afford shooting and all its other associated costs, you can afford safety glasses.

On one very memorable night during our winter league season, I was shooting my .22 target rifle in the prone position when a cartridge not just fired, but detonated in the chamber. As a result, I had brass particles from the disintegrated cartridge painfully impregnate the skin across the right half of my face. The force was such that some very small brass particles "welded" themselves to my glasses. Had it not been for my safety glasses, there was no doubt I would have needed immediate medical attention.

Keep in mind that most indoor ranges are in relatively remote settings. If I had been shooting alone at the time, how would I have accomplished all the normal things that needed to be done, or undone, when I go shooting? How would I have taken care of re-packing my equipment, locking up the range, or driving myself to the nearest medical facility, even if I knew where there was one? At the time that happened, I was sixty-three miles from home and unfamiliar with the nearby town. There's no doubt that the home team members would have taken care of me and my equipment if it came to that, but they shouldn't have to. When your eye suddenly has a hole in it, even a medical staff at the bench behind you is small consolation.

As it was, I was just shaken a bit by the event. After making sure that all the parts still worked, mine and the gun's, I continued the match with borrowed ammunition and the incident deeply etched only into my memory. Events like this can end a shooting career, or a profitable livelihood, or a visual world, faster than a blink. When it happens, you don't get any second chances. Normally, ejected brass cases are the least of the reasons for wearing glasses.

In my case, I was shooting factory loads in a factory condition gun. I had gotten a bad Lot of ammunition which the supplier readily replaced. But, no reason or excuse will give you the degree of COMFORT that safety glasses will. WEAR 'EM! Safety glasses are relatively inexpensive, so buy a pair for your shooting kit. The next time you leave home to go shooting and you say to your buddies or your family, "I'll see you guys later," you'll all have a reasonable expectation of it really happening.

Chapter Six
Vision and Vision Aids

Most of the world's better shooters can shoot with both eyes open without an eye-patch and have developed the ability to maintain a good sight picture in doing so. For some reason I haven't managed to acquire that ability.

Some shooters, including myself, have adopted the patch or a blinder to the non-sighting lens of our glasses that effectively allows sight down range to only our sighting eye when our head is in the shooting position. Without some type of left eye vision blockage, I

get double images of the sights sometimes, but only sometimes. It's that "sometimes" factor that is the distraction. To shoot without that distraction I painted the left side lens of a pair of cheap clip-on sunglasses and then used wire cutter pliers to clip off the right side lens. Now I have a clip-on, flip-up vision blocker that works great and allows me to shoot with both eyes open and still see the sights without thinking about it.

Dominic Zuccala displaying an example of a proper shooting stance.

Looking at the sights with one eye closed requires effort and that's why I wear the patch. A small piece of masking tape on the non-shooting lens will do just as nicely and can mean COMFORT for you.

The theory behind both eyes open is simple and reasonable. Since the muscles that control the eyelids when you blink are part of a sympathetic system, having one eye shut becomes an unnatural function. When you elect to close just one eye you work to override that system and that translates into a lessening, or an outright loss, of concentration. When only one eye is closed the other eye wants to close also, and the closed eye wants to open and as a result a flutter in the muscle of the eyelid of the closed eye may occur. When you become aware of the minutest tensions of such a condition you have just lost whatever COMFORT level you started with. The system really prefers to have both eyes open or both eyes closed. If you can't maintain a distinct, single image of the front sight with both eyes open for a continuous thirty seconds, patch it. Tape is cheap, and any residue from the tape can be cleaned from your lenses.

If the prescription in your glasses is so strong that a special lens in both sides would prevent you from performing the necessary chores associated with shooting, consider only one side, the shooting side as single vision and the other as bi or trifocal. This will allow you to perform all necessary tasks at the bench or the target while scoring and still allow you to focus on the front sight correctly.

There are devices on the market that you can either clamp onto the frames of your glasses or attach to the lens of your glasses by means of a suction cup that will greatly enhance your abilities to see the front sight. If you can already see the sights clearly, they will not improve your scores.

Some shooters use side shields on their glasses that help block out distracting light, or people, from the side. If you tend to be aware of motions near you as you try to shoot it might serve you well to try on a pair. I've seen shooters wear everything from modified playing cards to commercially produced signboards designed for this purpose. It's a matter of whatever works. What they do is cut a slit near each end of the card and then slide the temples of their glasses through the slits until the card protrudes slightly past the lens frame. In all cases, the material is stiff and will not flutter in the breeze.

Any glasses, or lenses, that diminish or intensify the light too much, should be avoided. Using amber or yellow lenses on overcast days may work well for you, but wearing them on bright, sunlit days can be harmful to your eyes. Sunglasses, or lenses, that diminish the contrast required for a crisp, sharp differentiation of the front and rear sights are also discouraged.

Notes

Chapter Seven
Hearing Protection

Before I was ten years old, I started shooting skeet regularly. I went to the Emmet County Sportsman Club skeet field near Harbor Springs, Michigan, every Sunday with my dad and several of my brothers and we would shoot four or five rounds of skeet at each outing. Back then, wearing hearing protection wasn't thought of as unmanly, it just wasn't a point of concern.

I remember that my father and one other gentleman wore rubber plugs that looked like little mushrooms. My father said that he wore them because the sharp reports of the shots hurt his ears. There was never any spoken suggestion that they might also keep him from going deaf. I guess that the unspoken assumption there was that if you could stand it, you didn't need ear protection. There was never any insistence, or encouragement, that the rest of us wear anything for ear protection. Because of that omission, today when listening to others talk, I make sure that my left ear is turned their way so I can hear everything. Also, at night, if the sounds around me are enough to keep me from getting to sleep, I turn over so that my

State trooper Tim Halvorsen displaying an example of a proper shooting stance.

left ear is on the pillow, effectively shutting out almost all of the noise.

Because of shooting without hearing protection over the decades, I have a significant hearing loss in my right ear. Even though I'm a right handed shooter, and because it's my right ear, I think it happened later in life while occasionally shooting larger caliber pistols without hearing protection.

In the shooting sports, hearing deficits are the number one injury. It's an insidious injury, one that doesn't manifest itself until you are older, usually much older and past the point of taking the necessary precautions. You won't get any second chances here, either. And unfortunately, you won't even know you missed the first chance until it's been squandered. Wearing hearing protection today sure beats turning up the volume on the TV, or learning to lip-read tomorrow. Ten bucks for a pair of earmuffs today is a lot cheaper than $1,800 for a hearing aid tomorrow.

Like the safety glasses, if you can afford to shoot, you can afford good hearing protection. A properly run range will require the wearing of muffs or sponge plugs while shooting is in progress whether you are participating or just an observer. I wear both and can hear everything I need to hear. For some reason my hearing actually improves slightly with the plugs in. WEAR HEARING PROTECTION!

Dr. Judy Tant, seven-time Women's National Pistol Champion, displaying her winning shooting stance.

The reason that I wear both types of protection is because of what is referred to as "startle response." I often found that as I was concentrating on my next shot I would have squeezed the trigger to a position right at its break point, but not quite, just as the person next to me fired his shot. The resulting shot report would sometimes startle me and cause my finger to twitch that needed extra thousandth of an inch, causing my gun to fire before it was my intention. Sometimes I was lucky, but most of the time I was not. Doubling the protection with plugs and muffs solved that problem for me. However, while using plugs and muffs together, I sometimes have to concentrate very hard to hear the commands of the match caller.

Good quality amplifying muffs (electronic) make shooting more enjoyable because they can be worn all the time you're on the range and you don't have to be worried about those surprise shots that always come while you're talking to someone. With amplifying muffs, you can talk and shoot with equal COMFORT.

Notes

Chapter Eight
Lighting

Ideal indoor lighting should come from overhead and behind the sights, and be bright but not glaring. The lighting at the bench should be enough to allow you to clearly see the front and rear sights, although that's not what you should clearly see when you are shooting. An explanation of that remark will follow later. Ideally, lighting down range should also be bright.

When you shoot out-of-doors the lighting is potluck, unless you are shooting under the lights, then the same desirable conditions apply. If you can't control the direction in which you shoot out-of-doors, you may want to wear an appropriate hat or baseball cap to shield your eyes from side or overhead light.

Indoors, a 100W bulb, a couple of feet above your head, should be sufficient. Proper lightning on your sights is vastly more important than proper or bright lighting on the target. You need enough light on the sights to see the front sight clearly. And when I say see, I mean SEE, not simply be aware of. If there were writing on the rear of the front sight blade, you should be trying to read it while you're lining up the front sight in the slot of the rear sight.

I have heard it said that some very good army shooters would first soot-blacken both the front and rear sights (as I do) then use a pocketknife to put a minuscule scratch in the center, top, backside of the front sight (the part of the front sight you see when sighting). That bright hairline scratch then becomes their concentration focal point during the entire match. All of your concentration should be at that same point. With your concentration totally on the front sight, the slot in the rear sight becomes a point of reference and awareness only, as it should be.

Since your entire body is already lined up perfectly on the target, all that's left is knowing where the front sight is. And since your visual focus is on the sharp and clear front sight, the rear sight and the target will become visibly fuzzy, blurred and indistinct. If that's the sighting picture you see when you're shooting with open sights, then that part of your shooting is correct.

If what you see is the front sight crisp and sharp, centered and level with the top of the indistinct rear sight slot and the black fuzzy ball of a target sitting quietly on top of the front sight, you are ready to make the gun go BANG. This sight position and picture is called a "Six o'clock hold." If you don't see this picture, you're not ready to make the gun go BANG, at least not inside the 10 or X rings, (if the gun is sighted in for a six o'clock hold). There are other shooters who position the top of the front sight in the center of the bull's-eye of the target, and this is called a "center hold." For some shooters the center hold works well. To me, the center hold requires that I qualify the exactness of the hold by moving the sight slightly to assure that I'm really still on center. In so doing, I'm moving the gun away from where I wanted it. This takes time and energy and doesn't make any sense to me. With the six o'clock hold, if a streak of white appears between the top of the front sight and the blurred black target, I can tell instantly that I'm holding low and I don't have to repeatedly qualify the hold.

It's been said that even a broken clock is correct twice a day. However, unlike the clock, the sights of a gun are always aligned on something. It's up to you to bring a correct alignment to bear on the target.

Practicing sight alignment techniques can be done safely and cost free. Paste a dot on the wall or on a piece of paper taped to the wall, and simply pull the trigger on your empty, or dummied, cocked pistol. You can do this at the range or in your house. Keep in mind, wherever you do it, ALWAYS treat your (any) gun as if it's loaded. Make sure that your friends, family, pets, are behind you. Besides, you don't need any distractions. So, until accidents become as extinct as dinosaurs, play it safe and you'll play longer. Also, you won't become extinct.

Notes

Chapter Nine
Breathing

At the very least, there are two schools of thought on the subject of proper breathing techniques. Mine and everyone else's.

The way I was taught to breathe while shooting pistols and rifles is to inhale through the nose, two or three moderately heavy breaths, and exhale them through the mouth (that I still do). Then I was told to let out half of the last breath and hold it there while I aligned the sights and fired the gun.

I have found through practice, and only for myself mind you, the two or three moderately heavy inhalations and exhalations to be acceptable, but I don't even try to hold any of the last breath. I let it all out. I don't force it out or push it out, I simply let my chest collapse on its own as much as it can, just as you would do with a deep and heavy sigh. The theory behind my method may seem a bit unusual, maybe even weird, but it works for me. As I see it, when a person dies the last physical action of the diaphragm, the muscle that causes a person to breathe, is to totally relax. It's a natural process and voids the lungs of any inner pressure, just as you do when you take a deep breath and sigh. Since the diaphragm is a muscle, why have it in a state of tension if it doesn't need to be? The only muscles that should be in a state of tension are those needed to keep your body vertical and your head up, those to support your arm and grip the gun, and those needed to pull the trigger.

Why a person takes a deep breath before they sigh is to acquire a condition and a sense of increased physical relaxation, or to get even more COMFORTABLE, if possible, even if only for a very short period. When I sigh deeply, that's precisely what I'm doing. Normally, for a few seconds after I sigh I don't need to breathe again anyway, and my chest stays collapsed and relaxed of its own volition. For a short period of time I don't even need to think about the amount of breath I've held, or should have held according to others.

The reasoning of the generally accepted method is that the small amount of oxygen left in the lungs is being absorbed into your system during the sighting and shooting period. You are, in effect, breathing without expanding your chest, thus giving you an extended period of time in which to sight, and shoot. That may be true, and I won't even try to argue the merits of it. I'm simply passing along what it is that's COMFORTABLE and works for me.

In slow fire I still accept the army's shooting team practice that if the shot isn't gone within about six seconds of acquiring my first best sight alignment, put the gun down, relax for a while, then start the entire cycle of concentration, breathing, sighting, and shooting, again.

Excessively heavy breathing (hyperventilating) to flood your system with oxygen will, unquestionably, do just that. However, by doing this, your heart rate jumps so high that your now pounding heart will negate the benefits of being able to hold your breath for a longer time. Any way you do your breathing for shooting purposes, develop a system of effective moderation. Closest to normal (for you) always works best.

Chapter Ten
Relative Shooting Position #1

Stand with your hands in your pants pockets and your feet placed about shoulder width apart. Your weight should be equally distributed to both legs and to both heels and the balls of your feet. This is a very familiar position for everyone because this is a standing position that we often assume when we can't sit and we are listening to, or are engaged in, interesting conversations. Take note of the position of your feet relative to the rest of your body. If you think about it, the reason your feet are where they are is because you are COMFORTABLE with them in that position. And that's also where they belong for one-handed pistol shooting. Whenever you take your shooting stance at the line, try to establish this feet-to-body relationship position. Remember, this is a position that you assumed without thought because it's natural for you. This is your Relative Shooting Position #1.

Making necessary line preparations just prior to a match.

At practice sessions when I was getting started in competitive shooting, I used a felt tipped marker (at the expense of some indelicate and derisive comments) to outline my shoes on the floor after I had gone through the procedure of establishing the "perfect" position for me. This can be a good training aid because you get used to the feel of repeating a productive position every time you come to the line. From day to day, or event to event, your feet positioning may change in small and subtle amounts due to refining your position each time you return to the line. Accept these changes. Don't get stuck on the notion that what was "perfect" the last time you shot should be a photocopy every time you step to the line. As time passes, your stance will appear to become a copy, and that's good, but don't belabor the point. A rapid acquisition of feet positioning when you step to the line will come to you in its own good time if you work at it.

The practice of outlining your feet on the floor or the ground, in any manner in competition is considered very unsportsmanlike conduct, and may, in fact, be against NRA sanctioned event rules. My advice to you is, if you think you need them, use the markings for practice only until such time that you don't need them anymore, and then just stop using them. Trust me, that time will come more quickly than you might think, if you practice a lot.

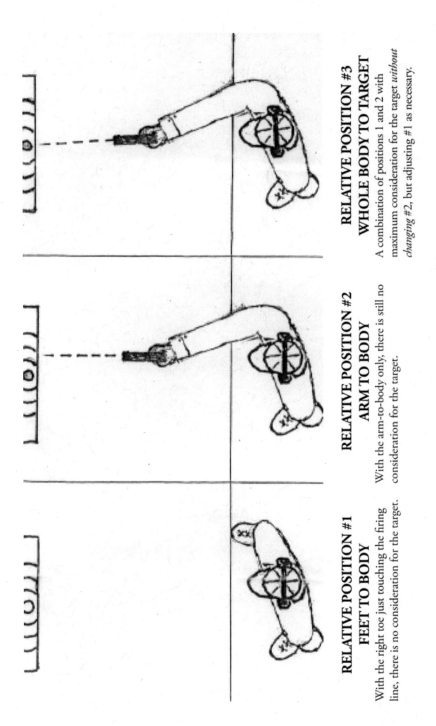

RELATIVE POSITION #1
FEET TO BODY

With the right toe just touching the firing line, there is no consideration for the target.

RELATIVE POSITION #2
ARM TO BODY

With the arm-to-body only, there is still no consideration for the target.

RELATIVE POSITION #3
WHOLE BODY TO TARGET

A combination of positions 1 and 2 with maximum consideration for the target *without* changing #2, but adjusting #1 as necessary.

Notes

Chapter Eleven
Relative Shooting Positions #2 & #3

For position two, pick out a small spot on the wall about eye level, or tack a piece of paper on the wall with a 3/8" black dot on it. Next, mark, tape or otherwise establish a "firing" line on the floor two yards from the wall, parallel to the wall. Put a large dot on that line 90 degrees from the center of the dot on the wall. You can use a plumb bob to establish the point on the floor from which to establish the 90 degrees. Now, with your shooting hand foot (right hand, right foot; left hand, left foot) forward, stand with the leading edge of your forward foot on the dot on the line and your body at about a fifteen to twenty degree angle to the line. This angled stance will change somewhat in the next step.

With your pistol in hand and properly gripped, and your non-shooting hand in your pocket or your belt and standing as relaxed and as COMFORTABLY as you can, close both eyes. While keeping your eyes closed, rotate your head to face the unseen target as if you were going to shoot at it. With your eyes still closed, raise your shooting arm to its most COMFORTABLE horizontal position and aim the gun at an as yet imaginary target. Don't be concerned about the dot on the wall just yet, although that will be your eventual goal. Right now, you shouldn't care if you're actually aiming anywhere close to the target.

Hold the gun up in your most COMFORTABLE shooting position for about thirty seconds. During this time your arm will probably (may) drift slightly to the left or the right as it seeks its own COMFORT zone without you using vision to make corrections. LET IT DO IT! Your arm is actually seeking to find where the least strenuous horizontal position is for your arm, your shoulder and your back muscles, those muscles used only for lifting and holding the gun. The muscles that control lateral motion of the arm should become more relaxed as your arm finds that "perfect" horizontal position. Don't fight the drift. Let your arm settle into whatever horizontal location it wants. Do this exercise three or four times and still don't be concerned about the target yet. Get used to the idea of your arm finding "Its Proper Place."

During this process, you are establishing the most natural horizontal position for your shooting arm relative to the rest of your body, just as you did with your feet. When you find that most COMFORTABLE arm position through repetitive trials you will also have found, Relative Shooting Position #2. The first RSP position was feet-to-body. This RSP position is arm-to-body. You're now ready to acquire position three.

Without changing the proper arm-to-body or feet-to-body positions, open your sighting eye. Right here, right now, what you do is super critical to any successes that you may enjoy, or dream about enjoying, as a pistol shooter. If you don't have a precise, or even a close sight picture with the dot on the wall sitting perfectly positioned atop your front sight, DON'T, and I repeat, DON'T move your arm horizontally to acquire perfect sight on target alignment. That is what second-rate shooters do, and that's a good part of the reason they are, and will remain, second-rate shooters.

When you lifted your arm and let it settle into its most COMFORTABLE shooting position, it settled into a position that now requires the fewest muscles doing the least amount of work, and that's good. In this position you are using only those muscles that are necessary to do what you are doing. If this is not that "perfect" sighting position you desire, you can't move your arm to the left or the right without forcing other groups of muscles to start working. If you do move your arm to the left or the right, those other muscles will, very shortly, be telling your brain "This is not feeling right, it's tiring, and we want to go back where we weren't working so hard." You have obviously moved outside those muscles COMFORT zone and they know it and they don't like it and they'll tell you so very soon.

If you insist on keeping your arm in that "corrected," forced and unnatural position, the concentration needed to do so will be stolen from the concentration you should be applying to the front sight to maintain sight alignment on the target. The energy needed to maintain that "correct" position will be taken from the energy you need to perform correctly. You can blame a few errant shots near the end of the match on something else, anything, but in reality it will probably have been fatigue that produced them. Neither a good shooter nor an improving shooter can afford to have anything other than 100% of his concentration focused on the front sight, so take the misused and unnecessary muscles out of the picture.

At this point, it can be pretty safely assumed that even if your sights are now aligned to each other, they are not horizontally lined up on the target. A remedy for this less than perfect condition is quite simple.

Imagine yourself as a toy soldier aiming a pistol. Your arms, your body, your legs and your feet are all solid and in fixed positions relative to each other, i.e. Relative Positions #1 and #2 are perfect. Also, imagine that you are standing on a large, rotatable flat disk. There is a line drawn from side to side through the center of the disk, and a marble sized dot on that line in the exact center of the disk. Place yourself on the disk with the toe of your front foot touching that dot and then reestablish those perfect, COMFORTABLE, Relative Positions #1 and #2.

Since you can't (shouldn't) change these relative positions to achieve a desired sight picture/alignment with the target, you have only one option left to you, and that is to rotate the imaginary disk until the desired sight alignment is achieved horizontally. In actuality this is not nearly as impossible as it sounds.

Instead of rotating the imaginary disk, which is now the floor or the ground, you need to rotate yourself, all of yourself, making sure that the tip of your toe touching the dot never leaves that touch point while you're rotating. You must pivot on the ball of the front foot and move only the back foot to the left or the right in an arc around the dot. Nothing about your Relative Positions one and two should change. What is changing is your relative position to the target of positions one and two, thereby acquiring your last Relative Shooting Position #3, the Total COMFORT Position.

In effect, what you did is rotate the whole toy soldier (you) so that its gun sights lined up on the target horizontally without bending anything in the process. The soldier is still in its original perfect condition and there are no signs of stress on any of the other parts of him. With the exception of maybe moving the gun up or down slightly and/or rotating your wrist slightly to align the sights vertically on the target, position-wise you're ready to shoot.

At this point, it should be understood that the gun may be very COMFORTABLE in your hand, but when you acquire the proper sight alignment you may have also acquired an improper grip. If that condition exists, you must either modify your muscular grip or slightly modify the material grips on the gun. In either case, you're going to have to reeducate some muscles.

Each time you need to move for a better horizontal alignment of the sights, close your eyes and repeat the COMFORT positioning routines. You may need to move your back foot four or five times before you get it right, and sometimes as little as an eighth of an inch. A minuscule clockwise or counterclockwise rotation on the balls of both feet at the same time, or just the back foot, will often accomplish just what you want for extremely small corrections. Sometimes it amounts to simply rocking up on your toes only to the point of breaking contact with the ground with your heels, then twitching your heels left or right and settling back down into your stance, with better alignment on the target. Don't hesitate to do it. Your scores will suffer for it later if you needed to do it and you dismissed it as a trivial or unnecessary adjustment. Remember, the bullet only has to touch the scoring rings to get the higher score. Quite often, the only difference between touch, and not touch is in the perception of the person scoring your target. It's your job to eliminate any misperception.

If your Total COMFORT position has been practiced often enough, you can use this technique to intentionally, and consistently, move bullet holes as little as half an inch at twenty-five yards, and when you get really good, at fifty yards. The foot movement can literally be as minuscule as wiggling your toes inside your shoes without moving the shoe. For such small adjustments you don't need to close your eyes. Just remember, it's always the back foot, or the rear wheel if you're in a wheelchair, that you should be moving for target-to-sight alignment. Once you find "the" position, do not move your feet again during all of your firing on that one target unless you absolutely have to. It's foolish to go through all that realignment process if you don't need to. Take advantage of anything that is a plus to your efforts. Finding correctness and maintaining it is a plus.

Another very important advantage to being correctly positioned on the line, is that when you bring the gun down or up on the target as you are aiming it, it will be on your own target (assuming you were on your own target to begin with). The chances of cross firing on your neighbor's target are greatly reduced if you have achieved your Total COMFORT Shooting Position.

These same principles also apply to rifle shooting in any of its many disciplines and positions, but there are also other elements to consider when shooting a rifle. A natural hold and COMFORT will help you have a less tiring day at the range.

As the above-discussed techniques pertain to pistol shooting, you may need to move just your wrist ever so slightly to get that perfect sight alignment. If you do, be very sure that it's only a wrist rotation or a vertical arm motion and not a horizontal arm movement. Once the horizontal positioning is established, some shooters prefer to come up on the target with the front sight when aiming while others prefer to come down on the target. Spend some time finding out which works best for you. A note of caution is worth mentioning here: If you do come down on the target, be extremely mindful of when and how much contact pressure you are applying to the trigger while the muzzle is still slightly elevated. A good practice is to apply no pressure other than trigger awareness pressure to the trigger, for correct trigger-to-finger location purposes, until the aligned sights cross into target backer or the white of the paper target. An "Oops" at this time could be disastrous for someone you may never see and have far-reaching and lifelong or life-ending ramifications.

Let's try a hypothetical situation here. Suppose someone shows up with a big truck and it's full of silver dollars. Then they tell you you can take those dollars out of the truck, and you get to keep all the silver dollars you threw (one at a time) through a 3" knothole in a board fence that's eight feet away from you, but only for the next two days, and, if you accept the offer, you are obligated to throw at least one coin every minute for twelve hours of each of those two twenty-four hour periods. Also, for each dollar you throw that does not go through the knothole they get to keep, plus, you must give them back two dollars. But, for every ten dollars that you collect you get a ten dollar bonus. Even with the bonus offer, there's a real possibility that you may wind up throwing your own money at the knothole. Knowing that time is running out, how much concentration and analysis of body-language and position and throwing force, and in general, what you're trying to accomplish, would you apply to this challenge? And how long do you think it would take you to perfect your most profitable stance and technique? That is exactly what successful shooting is like.

Winners have practiced untold hours of just what is necessary to get the silver dollars to go through the knothole on purpose, and it's the winners that always go home with most of the silver dollars. They don't practice anything that has second place, or almost, associated with it. The mental conditioning they nurture and carry with them tells them repeatedly that they are winners and that they will win. The only competition that winners have is within themselves, and that leads us to the next chapter.

Notes

Chapter Twelve
Attitude and Mental Conditioning

Your first and foremost concern under this heading is a safety issue. NEVER leave a functional, shootable gun unattended whether it's loaded or unloaded. If you are going to be away from its control, even momentarily except at a rules conducted match, check it to be sure that it's empty and unloaded and then put it in your shooting box, pistol sleeve or lock it up where no one can get to it. It should never be out of your sight control. At a match, the range safety officers will be the attendants that watch over your equipment. They are not responsible for it. They simply watch it and make sure the shooting line remains safe while scoring is being done.

Secondly, in a non-match situation, KNOW what is down range at, and behind, the target area and well beyond that to what could become the bullets impact area if you overshoot the backstop. This is no time to guess or to assume anything incorrectly. Once you squeeze that trigger, you could be altering your future, or someone else's. GUN SAFETY IS NO ACCIDENT. GUN SAFETY IS AN ATTITUDE. To what degree you implement it is a sign of your maturity.

As in all information that comes to us, it must be filtered, reviewed, and digested before it becomes useful, usable, and we get the greatest benefit from it. Not all that we see and hear, or even read, is necessarily applicable to our goals. This is where the character of a shooter emerges and is tested repeatedly. Acceptance of valid, useful information and the rejection of detrimental information will help enable the improvable shooter to improve. Until you have seen, heard and recognize many of the positive qualities of good marksmanship, are serious about understanding them and diligently practicing and applying them to your benefit, you are destined to fail to improve to the level of shooting to which you may aspire. Desire never got anybody anything. Only work works.

When I speak of competition I am speaking of a contest or display of talents and abilities between two or more persons which results in an accumulation of points or numbers by the contestants, the winners generally being the person(s) with the most points. i.e. the person most capable of capitalizing on his/her training, talent, focused discipline and abilities with the highest degree of success. Competition is the event in which you participate. Competition is something which should remain personal or within your mind. You should not be concerned with the other shooters and their fabled or unknown abilities. If you were doing it correctly, each time you practiced you were striving to perform with increased ability. There was no one there to "beat." You were trying to acquire and perfect proven techniques that would add to your own abilities and talents. Scores should have been of no concern, or at the most, a secondary consideration.

When you enter a shooting "competition" or event, keep in mind that there MUST NOT BE ANY competition within your thinking. All you should be trying to do is applying the principals and techniques that you know are correct and that you have practiced, and try to improve over your own past best scores, one shot at a time. Realistically, that's all you can do or expect to do. Let's face it, you are not going to jump from Sharpshooter to Master and Match winner in one afternoon. Be justifiably proud and satisfied with being a few points better, for a known reason, each time you compete as a result of not "competing" with yourself.

All the champions of the world have been through the mental process of accepting only the workable elements in their fields of expertise. They also know, and understand, what causes—not simply allows—failure, and they focus only on what is necessary to become successful. Since they already know that the negative things won't work, they don't clutter up their thinking or their actions with them. Besides, they can't concentrate in more than one direction at a time any better than you or I. They are champions because they think like champions and are always aware that their physical abilities alone will not sustain them.

A very important facet of the negative side of shooting is mental aggression. Whether it's becoming upset with your own performance or with the people and things around you, dwelling on things that you should have addressed earlier, or situations over which you have absolutely no control, will always be counterproductive. Things do go wrong! You will make "dumb" mistakes! When things start going wrong for you on the line, it's very easy to react to them by becoming a little upset, or even angry. If your mental reaction to "situations" is anything more than momentary, or a simple acknowledgment, your reaction has become much more than a simple negative element in your mental approach to the match. It has become a negative retreat, a withdrawal from the ideal, and a step backward from a feeling of COMFORT that you may have had just a few moments earlier. Reacquiring that COMFORT will always take more time and mental energy than you can afford.

If you are capable of the quality of shooting that you came to the range to do, try thinking of the distractions that pop up (and there will be many) as a test of your own mettle and character. What is the real inner quality of the stuff of which you are made?

Are anger and frustration the most well-polished tools in your toolbox? Are they your best qualities, qualities that produce the most rewarding results? Those should be absurd questions, but they are ones that may help you cultivate qualities that are more useful and worthwhile, qualities that will more readily help you achieve your desired goals.

Such a situation is a chance for you to triumph over COMFORT-killing anger and the loss of productive concentration by refusing to be denied your goals. If a burr gets under your saddle before a match, take care of it before the match. If it gets under there during a match, address it after the match. Learn to take care of "things" at the proper time. At any given match, there are already enough frustrated shooters on the line. You don't need to join their ranks.

Here's a wild and totally unrealistic example of what I'm talking about. Just think about it for a while.

Just suppose that you have ninety-plus rounds of ammo in your pockets, enough for a one gun match, and you have just fired your third shot at fifty yards, the slow fire stage of the match. You're focused and you've really got it together today. Those first three shots are 10s and the high probability of one being an X. You obviously have an accurate gun, your mind is in the right place, the ammo is good, your skill level is certainly not in question, your stance is perfect, and you feel great. You're on your way.

From out of nowhere, two guys, with more tattoos than they have skin for, orange spiky hair, and enough piercings and rings on their bodies that if they laid down on a flotation device in a pond, they'd point north and south, suddenly show up with blaring boom boxes slung under their arms. They pick up your shooting bench and walk off with it, gun box, scope, and all. Now, apart from the fact that they aren't going to steal any of it, (but you don't know that) and you desperately want to freak out, what have they done that has changed your ability to reacquire your sight picture on the target, or your ability to shoot eighty-seven more 10s or Xs? Not a thing. Nothing. Nada. So, if you can learn to ignore those score-killing distractions and remain cool and focused on your goal, you will prevail, not the detractors.

In competitive shooting, it's not unheard of for someone to intentionally try to get your goat, to give you something unimportant and inconsequential to think about just to throw you off your game. It may be beguilingly subtle, or it may not be and you can't prove their intent in either case. But if you fall for it, it's too late to analyze it. They've won and you've lost.

We call these "head games," and the people that resort to such ploys, in serious competition, display serious and glaring character flaws as well as an obvious lack of sportsmanship. They also lack a true confidence in their own, possibly very good, abilities. And, while they may have posted the winning scores of the match, those individuals have never been, and will never be, winners.

Shooters assembling for a match.

Protocol and manners go hand-in-hand with attitude. You should be more aware of your own behavior than that of others. Think about what you are doing. Don't intentionally do or say anything at the range that will diminish or negatively affect the abilities of others or yourself. If you can't win because of your own shooting ability, you rightfully don't deserve to win.

Under the heading of detrimental personal qualities, or excess baggage, are two very common entries. One is praise, or the lack of it, and the other is criticism. They are two sides of the same coin, and either, or both, can be very damaging to your scores if you fail to handle them correctly.

Not getting praise (deservedly so, or not) can be considered a form of unspoken criticism. If you're the type of person that seeks praise, you may not do very well until you get some. If, however, you understand that most people offer praise where praise is due, and you recognize it as nothing more than that when you get some, you'll probably take it in stride, say "Thanks," and get on with the next step in your shooting evolution. Don't expect praise when you perform well. After all, that's what you're supposed to do, isn't it? On the other hand, when you do get that well-earned praise and pat on the shoulder, learn how to accept it graciously and use it to your benefit, if you haven't already.

Ninety-nine percent of the time, constructive criticism should not be considered a personal attack on your character. However, this can be another of those times when your character is tested. How criticism was presented to you, who gave it to you, and under what circumstances it was given to you all contribute to its perceived validity. What credence or value you give to it, how you react to it and what you do with it, if anything, have a bearing on your development as a shooter (and life in general). And likewise, here, you must learn to use criticism as a tool to your benefit just as you do with praise. If, in your competitive shooting career you received no praise or criticism at all, it would probably be because no one was really concerned about you one way or the other, and you would grow more slowly as a shooter. You need input. Input is a healthy thing.

The time it took you to read that last paragraph is more time than you should take dwelling on the subject. Keep in mind: people like yourself have a lot on their minds, too. People forget. Cut them and yourself some slack.

Extend your own thanks and congratulations to other shooters freely when it's deserved. Offering whatever assistance you can to help someone else improve their skills is a common trait among good shooters. Everyone, and the sport as a whole, is the better for it. Fortunately in the sport of shooting, there's an abundant supply of qualified shooters out there to give you a pat on the back and a "well done," every time it's deserved. If you ask for it, those same people will be just as willing to help you figure out, or just flat out tell you, what you're doing wrong and give you a tip or two to help you get through it and get it right. When you find people like that, pick their brains until they start to run away at the sight of you. Learn to use (as opposed to abuse) them graciously as tools for your benefit. Listen to the advice of better shooters than yourself whether you like them or not. Just because you don't like someone, doesn't mean you can't benefit and learn from him or her. You may not like the banker, but he's the guy with all the money. Imagine how close the results of a battle (the next match?) would be if you had the same knowledge the "enemy" has.

Read everything you can about the techniques used by successful shooters and learn to separate the wheat from the chaff for your own gain. As you learn more and shoot better, the overall standards of the sport of shooting also rise.

Keep in mind that there are no strings attached to the bullets you are shooting. You can't pull them back before they hit the paper in the wrong spot and shoot them again, but this time where you meant to shoot. They're gone. Forget them. If you were doing your best when the gun went BANG, just your knowing that simple fact should be satisfaction enough for the time being. Becoming upset, even a little bit for any reason, will steal pieces of your positive concentration, and positive concentration is hard enough to harness and focus without throwing it away to a lost cause.

From the first shot of the match to the last shot, concentrate on your own target. When doing the scoring, try to avoid making comparisons with your neighbor's or your friend's targets or developing a sense of how you are doing compared with the rest of the field. If the match is not over, you still haven't done your best, and that's all you're supposed to be trying to do. If you're not in the position of being caught, score-wise, you're putting yourself under unnecessary pressure and you probably won't catch up, either.

Instead of dwelling on a possible momentary misjudgment, think only of the next shot because, when you stop to think about it, all there is in the sport of shooting is next shots. If you refrain from adding up the values of shots as you go along, and concentrate on what needs to be done to make your next shot the shot you desire, the score will take care of itself. The most obvious and self-fulfilling rewards are the personal achievements of individual performances and successes that all individual sports provide. Success in shooting is a result of your own efforts. No one else can shoot a 10 or an X for you.

Image of serenity that helps my mental relaxation.

If you're fortunate to become involved in team shooting and team competition, you will immediately feel the joys of being a contributor to the team. When you do well the whole team does well, and when the team does well, it comes back on you and you will do better. You and the team evolve and grow together because of each other. That same philosophy applies to the cultivation of friendships among any group of responsible shooters.

If you are going to the range for practice or a competitive match go with one thought in mind, to do your utmost to do what is necessary to score as high as you can, and that doesn't mean all your shots at twelve o'clock in the six ring either. Even in wanting levity there's a difference between high scores and winning scores.

The attitude that you bring to the range is probably the most important and useful tool you can have and is the major contributor, by far, to your shooting successes. A positive, educated, and relaxed attitude is the most required and should be the most polished and used tool in your "tool box." Like any other job worth doing if you haven't brought well-maintained tools with you, you will struggle and you will not get the job done.

If you study and learn and maintain a positive attitude it will eventually translate into higher scores (albeit slowly) because you'll be more able to readily perform the tasks needed to allow you to shoot better. You'll be much closer to "having your act together," and not having to try putting it together at the last minute. If you practice or compete with a less than positive attitude, you're probably harboring subtle and destructive excuses about why things aren't going exactly your way. On closer examination, you'll find that the reasons for your imperfection and your excuses for imperfection don't match.

There is no argument that it takes less mental and physical energy to place 2nd, 3rd, or 4th in a match than it does to be the winner. If you're competing against "the better shooters" or someone who possesses "natural ability," whatever that is, you'll need an even tighter focus and a greater assurance of your own abilities. This is the time to concentrate on all the correct things that you learned and need to do and then set about doing them.

If you're shooting at a target with a 10 or an X as the bull's-eye, actually think . . . 10 . . .10 . . .10 or X . . . X . . . X as you align your sights on the target. If you're willing to accept shots in the 9, 8, or 7 rings, or less, that's what you'll shoot most of the time. When the gun fires, use your mind's eye to actually track or steer the bullet down range right into the bull's-eye and keep telling yourself that it's 10, X, or nothing. Demand 10s and Xs of yourself.

Within the realm of mental conditioning is something we call, "follow-through." Follow-through consists of such things as the following items: The retention and continuance of your best grip after a shot is fired. Your trigger finger still trying to come straight rearward despite the fact the gun has just fired. Your sighting eye remaining focused on that point in space where the front sight was at the instant of discharge (and to which it will return). Your reestablishing the pistol's sight alignment back on the target. Your arm remaining positively extended and locked and your head staying locked in your shooting position while your entire body stays in the ready to shoot posture. In other words, for about one second after the gun fires there must be no physical relaxation in the intensity of your body's collective effort to hit the bull's-eye, especially between the shots in timed and rapid fire. Intensity does not mean muscle tightness or the need for greater strength. In this case, intensity means a focus on details.

There is no doubt about it, this is a lot to ask of your body, particularly for a new shooter. You must think of each one of these follow-through conditions as a part of a single equation for a single action. Which part can you leave out and still get the right answer? None of them! Not one of them is more or less important than the others, and none of them will reward you without the joining and blending of all the others, because they are all equal and all necessary for the desired results.

In the timed and rapid-fire stages of a match all of those points are absolutely necessary for a minimum span of twelve to twenty-two seconds and if you relax just a little or fail to do any one of them your next shots most likely won't be where you want them to be. You can't hope ten shots into the bull's-eye and no winner ever hoped his or her way to a championship. Someone once said that Joe Louis never would have been the world heavyweight boxing champion if he hadn't had fifty or sixty lucky punches in every fight. Let's face it, luck had no part in it. Joe was well prepared before he showed up.

In professional golf and baseball the champions, the control hitters, have spent countless hours developing, practicing and honing correct follow-through because they understand its importance to their game and its necessity for achieving eventual success. They understand that what happens in the after contact portion of their swing, is as super-critical and necessary as is the precision and correctness in the before contact portion of their swing.

The same is true with shooting. To fire shots into the 10 and the X rings repeatedly what you do to control the gun and prepare for the next shot is just as necessary and demanding as what happens before the hammer falls. And all of it needs to be done exactly the same again and again and again until the last shot has been fired and the match is over.

There is only one true and exact line of momentum leading up to the successfully resultant contact with a golf ball or a baseball. The same is true while squeezing the trigger of a gun that results in sear disengagement and hammer fall and a shot into the 10 ring. And because of the laws of physics, there is momentum because of the swinging motions or the squeezes of triggers, i.e. follow through. The short time lines before and after the hammer starts to move must be of equally correct precision.

If you tried to hit a home run or a hole-in-one but gave up trying to maintain the bat or the club momentum at the very instant of contact with the ball, you'd never come close to achieving your goal. This is also true with your trigger squeeze and sight alignment. You must follow through as if the shot hasn't occurred yet. When those other fellows say, "Man, I sure hit that ball right," they're talking about attitude, grip, stance, equipment, and the motion of the club or bat from the moment it starts to move from address until it completes its follow-through.

You may wonder how there can be such a thing as follow-through when the trigger of your gun may not even travel a 32nd or a 64th of an inch after discharge. In our case follow-through is not a wide sweeping arc with great body and equipment motion, but rather a sense of continuance of what is needed to intentionally and repeatedly hit the bull's-eye.

Part of the mental conditioning for successful shooting involves frequently living and reliving all these aforementioned points in your mind. When your mind is not otherwise occupied with running your life, run these points through it. You can do it while you're walking down the street, driving home from work, taking a shower, mowing the lawn, washing the dishes, trying to get to sleep or whatever other time your mind is otherwise available.

These repetitive thoughts away from the range can greatly reduce your need to try to recall them when you do step to the line. As a result some, or all of them, will become automatic conditioned responses sooner rather than later, and that's one or two fewer things unanchored and floating around in your head to affect your concentration.

Another thing that is probably the biggest monkey on the back of the newer shooter in competition is "match jitters," or nervousness. At one time or another they've gotten to all of us. They're just part of paying your dues in the shooting game. As you attend more matches and become more familiar with the routine of match procedures, they will continue to diminish until you'll wonder what

all the fuss was about. For the most part, having match jitters is a matter of wanting to do well in front of the good shooters or friends and/or a fear of doing something glaringly stupid that will embarrass you. If you continue with productive practices both concerns will take care of themselves rather quickly. A positive aspect of match jitters is that it's a sign, sometimes a too evident sign, that you care about what you're doing, and that's worth something.

In the same category as match jitters are the, "success jitters." There are those people that can't handle success very well and here I'm not talking about poor sportsmanship.

Case-in-point; Joe is shooting the slow fire portion of the match and on his first target. He has fired six shots in a row within the 10 ring. Until now, Joe has never

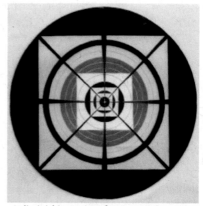

A diminishing point of concentration with a target within a target within a target

even come close to this accomplishment. As the 10s accumulate, the excitement and the tension inside Joe builds rapidly. When he looks in the scope to see where number six hit he practically comes unglued with elation. When he brings the gun up for number seven he may as well be swatting flies with it, and it looks like he is. There's no chance of him putting the last four shots where they could and should go. It's not a matter of, "Can Joe do it?" He is doing it. Joe has simply exposed himself to evidence of a higher level of his skill that hasn't surfaced before now. He's on a new plateau, one that he's worked hard for, one that's now suddenly welcoming him unexpectedly. He's become very excited and nervous in his recognition of it, and the fact that others are now going to also recognize it. Joe is in new and uncharted territory. His problem is not a fear of failing with the next four shots, it's being able to, unexcitedly or objectively, accept the success that he's rightfully earned and worked so hard for.

Joe needs to remember that he came to the match to intentionally place shots inside the 10 or the X ring. He knows he's capable of it as his practicing and this target has proven. At such a time as this objectivity must hop onto Joe's shoulder and whisper in his ear, "This is why you came here, isn't it?" and "This isn't the first new thing you've ever learned to handle, so let's get on with it."

That looks and sounds great and very philosophical in print on these pages, but let me assure you that it's nowhere near as easy as I make it sound here, not by a long shot (pun intended). Reducing or eliminating match and/or success jitters is a time consuming learned process helped by productive practices that result in slowly elevating your scores. It's definitely not something you're going to talk yourself out of between shots. Losing match jitters is an "acquired taste" and acquiring that loss requires a lot of hard work on your part because it's not free and it's not easy.

One thing that would have aided Joe is not looking in his scope after the first two shots if he knew they were where he called them. Once you can establish that your gun is doing what you expect it to do under unchanging conditions, forget the scope. Fire each shot as best you can and rely on your call. If your gun is doing its job, and your shot calls are right, the scope won't make the score a bit better. However, as in Joe's case, the scope can make things a lot worse.

In the same context of mental disruptions is an event that took place at Camp Perry, Ohio, during the National Pistol Matches in the summer of 1980. This was my first trip to the matches. I was as green as they come. Shooting next to me was a fatigue-uniformed military gentleman of very high skill, but I didn't know that at the start of the match. As the match progressed along smoothly a robin-sized bird flew across the range and perched on the top of his target frame. I saw it there and it immediately became a matter of humor to me. I had visions of a small cloud of feathers slowly drifting to the ground. (I do not need any letters.)

The bird was on his target frame but it was I who was being affected by it. His scoring started high and remained high and I doubt if he ever would have commented about the bird if I hadn't brought it up to him as we walked down to score the targets. His only reply to my mention of it was an expressionless, "Yeah, I saw it."

Because I was entertaining the vision of that bird as I was trying to shoot, I was obviously not applying the necessary concentration to the task at hand. I probably could have dug up some reasons for what I had done, but I sure didn't have any good excuses. I knew better than to be thinking sophomoric at a time like that. How I scored that day is immaterial. What is material is that one of us had trained himself to concentrate on the job at hand the way it needed to be done and the other, me, was wasting the moment by allowing outside and irrelevant forces to dictate my performance.

Unintentionally I had become a detractor, and this guy wasn't falling to it. He remained focused on his goals. I think he must have read something like this. He may not have been the match winner that day but he surely conducted himself like one. More importantly, I had become my own biggest detractor, not something that I can ascribe to the "smart move" column.

When you shoot out-of-doors don't be surprised if such things happen. Think of them as events unworthy of your attention and train yourself to work around them. As outrageous an example as it was, remember the shooting bench that walked away.

Objectivity is another quality that is necessary to your growth as a shooter. It can be a complicated tool to understand and master, but fortunately, its use becomes easier with the acquisitions of knowledge and acquired skill. These three qualities require each other's support, always. If you can see the sights correctly, the gun is accurate and functions properly and it fits you, accept that viewpoint and, if necessary, act on it accordingly, few of those shortcomings will remain with you for long.

The last thing under this heading is tricks and gimmicks. If you've ever been in a gun store or to a gun show, you've seen all the trinkets and gadgets available to "assist" you in hitting the target. Take my word for it, if the gun you have is accurate, functions properly and fits you, you've got all the necessary "other" equipment you're ever going to need right between your ears. That's where winning scores come from.

Notes

Chapter Thirteen
Physical Fitness (Conditioning)

Your physical condition is reflected in your scores, also. Poor physical condition can be, but is not limited to, any of the following: Inability to hold the gun correctly on target for twenty-five to thirty seconds without starting to tremble, poor eyesight or glasses that need correcting, not enough nourishment, too much of the wrong foods consumed before a match, including caffeine, chocolate, or alcohol (for any reason), and foods that may cause gas or acid stomach (heartburn) or a lingering bad taste in your mouth. The use of tobacco in any form should be avoided.

When you're about to touch off the first shot of a five shot string in rapid fire and you're suddenly reminded of what you had for breakfast or lunch, your concentration goes right out the window. None of those condition deficits will allow you to get in, or stay in, your COMFORT zone. When the match is over you shouldn't have to say, "I was beaten by a chili dog." My shooting gear always includes a generous supply of antacid tablets and a small bottle of water.

The proper amount of sleep before a match is also necessary to stave off fatigue and keep your senses sharp. Remember, all candles were meant to be burned at one end only.

If you're traveling a long distance to a match that day, be sure that you arrive in plenty of time to recover from any driving fatigue or stiffness incurred en route. Before you are called to the firing line, do some stretching to work out the kinks. Allow yourself time to relax to regain as much of the normal COMFORT you had when you left home.

Limit yourself to the amount of liquids you drink just before matches. Include a small bottle of water as part of your match gear. Take it to the line with you so you can have a sip of water if you need it. Be sure that you use the restroom before the shooting begins. If you don't you could be reminded of failing to do so at the most inopportune moment. Again, you don't want to have to say, "I was beaten by a..." well, you get the picture.

If you alter or upset your normal daily routine too severely it will affect your ability to maintain the necessary concentration level you need. When I was shooting with an Army Reserve team, I would forego the morning coffee and the cigarettes until after the day's match and not really miss either, or so I used to like to tell myself. In that respect I was living a lie. Back then I loved to smoke pipes, cigars, cigarettes, and dearly loved that morning shot of caffeine with my breakfast. Not even barely hidden in my mind was the knowledge that when the match was over I could have a cigarette and a cup of coffee. I did shoot better without the coffee and the cigarettes, but I was still thinking about them from time to time and I was eager to get back to them. That day's routine had changed too severely for me.

Now, having said all that, I know a chain-smoking coffee drinker that shoots Masters scores with a .22 in the four position, indoor winter league matches, and he does this just before he goes to the line. However, Tom's control is the exception rather than the rule. He is able to demand from his system the focus necessary for the task at hand, and he gets the results he wants. He is thinking like a winner, not a, "hope to be a winner." Nothing about his routine had changed. How long he'll be able to keep that up is another matter entirely.

Wean yourself off caffeine days before a big match since the effects of caffeine withdrawal are a detriment. The same holds true for the nicotine from any source.

If you're taking prescription medicines that may have side effects that will affect your ability to score well, don't stop taking your medicine on match days just for the sake of your shooting. Your health is more important (to all of us) than a perfect score. However, if scores are the driving force in your shooting see your doctor about a modified or different prescription that will have less of an effect on you.

If what you consume won't let you be at 100% of your good health maybe you shouldn't be handling firearms in the first place. Avoid any medications that may impair your reflexes and detract from your ability to perform at your capable best. For safety's sake, remember: your scores aren't the only things on the line that can be hurt by a medically induced momentary lapse in judgment.

Whenever you eat something that may come back to bite you when you can least handle it, you've brought along excess baggage that you can't get rid of simply by relaxing or concentrating harder. For all intents and purposes, you brought a monkey to the match, he's on your back and he's all yours.

Some shooters carry a rubber ball or a wad of exercise putty or spring grips in their cars that they squeeze while driving for exercise to strengthen and improve their grip. As they drive around, they massage the ball or the putty or flex the spring gripper. Another good exercise is to spread out a full sheet of the daily newspaper on the table. Then, with only the shooting hand, wad it up into as tight a ball as possible, as fast as you can. Try that with the whole edition and I can guarantee that you won't fill even a small wastebasket very quickly.

Chapter Fourteen
Match Preparations

It is assumed, or it should be, that when you step up to the firing line and take your shooting stance you have everything you need, mentally and physically, that's necessary to allow you to fire a single shot into the bull's-eye, at twenty-five or fifty yards. Your gun is clean, accurate and you know how to shoot it. You have enough ammunition, your ear muffs/plugs are in place, your clothes are COMFORTABLE, your stance is correct, your glasses are clean, you can see the sights clearly, and you know which target is yours. You are thinking X or 10 and your grip is right. The most accurate ammunition you can find/afford is in your clips and the chamber, and your trigger finger is placed correctly, allowing you to slowly squeeze the trigger straight rearward while maintaining proper sight alignment. All that's needed now is the command to fire the gun.

It has been said that hitting the bull's-eye is simply a matter of pulling the trigger to the rear without disturbing sight alignment until the gun fires. The practice necessary to repeatedly and consistently achieve this condition at will is as demanding as doing it on the firing line in competition.

Be as prepared as you can be before you lift the gun to shoot it. Stepping to the line at a match is like jumping out of the airplane in skydiving. This is not the time to question the packing of your chute. Make up a checklist and use it to prevent forgetting things, things that if absent will steal your concentration. Have a small oil can and a small screwdriver handy during practice sessions and matches in case you need to adjust the sights or add a little lubrication to the slide. You shouldn't have to rummage through your equipment looking for such things while you're trying to shoot. Such gestures are concentration robbers.

Be sure that you take enough ammunition to the line to allow for your needing to fire at least two personal five shot alibi strings, plus the remote possibility of several five shot range alibi strings. Have your extra clips loaded and within easy reach of your non-shooting hand and make sure that they all have the requisite five rounds in them. To minimize that concern, since the manufacturer didn't do it, I've taken a sharp scribing tool and placed a very evident scratch on the side of my clips where the fifth round is when the clip is loaded. With that scratch all I need is a quick glance at the clip to assure myself that the clips are correctly loaded and ready.

In competition when the command to load is given, you insert the loaded clip into the gun and let the slide forward of its own volition. It is generally assumed that you have also just inserted a live round into the chamber and you are ready to shoot...but...just maybe... you're not. On more than one occasion, even good shooters have made that same logical assumption and been wrong. A good habit to get into after you release the slide is to pull it back again just far enough to see the brass of the cartridge in the crack. If there is brass in the crack crisply return the slide to battery. If there is no brass in the crack, pull the slide back and watch the first round being picked up from the clip and inserted into the chamber by the slide as it's returning to battery.

In the Timed and Rapid-fire stages of a match, you are allowed one five shot alibi string for each stage for the failure of your gun not to fire for reasons not of your own making. Not having a round in the chamber is your fault, and if it should happen to you, you will not be given an alibi string. Under such circumstances, by rule, after the command to fire has been given in a non-alibi string of fire, once you even touch any part of the gun in an attempt to correct your oversight, or for any other reason, you automatically forfeit any right to be allowed an alibi string. So, since you came to shoot, make sure you can. In an alibi string of fire you are allowed to clear malfunctions within the ten or twenty seconds, but unless you realize what has happened soon enough and reach up and manually recycle the slide you may have to forfeit anywhere from ten to fifty points.

If you have been allowed an alibi string, make sure that you check your magazines to ensure that they have five rounds in them. It's always good to have extra full magazines available for just such occasions. Set the extracted partially-full magazine aside and shoot the full ones. After the alibi string you can refill all of them at one time to ensure their readiness for the rest of the match.

If you're shooting out-of-doors and the wind is blowing dust around, keep your clips and ammunition under some kind of protective cover until you need to reload. The dust that manages to get into your gun's action and the barrel while you're actually shooting is bad enough without compounding the problem by putting dirty ammo in the clips. A little dirt in the bore of your otherwise accurate gun will start your scores downward despite your best efforts. On such days, run a dry cleaning patch through the barrel as often as is practical. During any extended delays and while you're down range scoring, place a towel over your guns or close your box to prevent dust from getting into the actions. Be very careful to not smudge the blacking you've so carefully applied to your sights.

If you're using a scope to spot your shots, have it lined up on your own target, focused and positioned closely enough to you that you don't need to move your feet even the slightest to use it effortlessly.

If the shooting distance is fifty feet or fifty yards, take every ethical and legal advantage they will allow you. Stand as close to the shooting line/bench while shooting as you possibly can without touching the bench. Touching the bench while you are shooting is against the rules and grounds for disqualification.

If there are rocks or spent cases on the ground that will affect how you stand, move them out of the way and find the best possible and most COMFORTABLE footing you can.

Before you go down range to score targets be sure that everything of yours on the firing line is ready for you to resume shooting the moment you return. If you're still down range or on your way back the range officials can plainly see that you're not ready to shoot. However, if you're back and not ready for whatever reason, they can't always tell that you're not ready and they will rightfully assume that shooting should resume despite how obvious your lack of preparedness may appear to you. Moreover, because you may be holding up the match, you will probably feel somewhat obligated to hurry and now you have introduced one more element into your shooting that is stealing your concentration. Fill all your clips, oil the slide, adjust your scope or your sights or whatever else needs adjusting before you leave the line to score the targets. The target and the person whose target you're scoring will still be down range when you get there. Look out for number one first. You're the only one at the match who will.

As a final note in this chapter, get yourself a copy of the latest NRA rules for your particular shooting discipline and become familiar with them. It could save you a lot of questions and a lot of heartache. In competitive shooting, you are obligated to know the rules before you step to the line and start shooting.

Chapter Fifteen
Practicing

How and what you practice is what you will become. If you practice mistakes, whether through ignorance or carelessness, you will perform mistakes at matches. What you carry to the firing line is the only thing you have going for you to work with and that includes what's inside your head, right or wrong, as well as all the physical things that you may do that can affect you.

Under the PRACTICING heading is a sub-heading of extreme importance called, "hammer-fall." When the hammer of your pistol (internal or external) falls, it should be a surprise to you. I'm not saying that you shouldn't know, within about five milliseconds when it will fall. I'm saying that you shouldn't know precisely when it will fall. Through endless hours of practicing your trigger squeeze you will get a very good feel for when the hammer will/should fall, but if the parts in your gun are made correctly, are clean and properly lubricated, you should never know with an absolute certainty just when the hammer will fall, ever. The best shooters have honed their tactile senses so finely that the difference between "about to fall," and actual hammer-fall finger pressure is so infinitesimal that, for all intents and purposes, there is no difference. For them it's not an unexpected surprise. Nevertheless, even to them, hammer- fall is and must be a surprise, educated or not.

If you can consciously and repeatedly determine when the hammer will fall, you are bringing into play a host of undesirable qualities that must be gotten rid of for you to succeed as a shooter, not the least of which is anticipating the shot and the recoil. The tendency is to react to them before they happen because you know they're coming, and in doing so your scores will reflect the tensing of the muscles normally used in that action. Knowing when the hammer will fall is a matter of subconscious awareness and as such it's something that shouldn't be on your mind while you're trying to focus only on sight alignment, as you must.

When you can predetermine when the hammer will fall, when squeezed correctly, you are accepting and nurturing in your shooting discipline the notion that you will tell the gun when to go "Bang." If you accept that notion, you will try to "dress up the shot." That means that when you have that almost perfect sight picture you will try to make it "juuussst" a little more perfect. In doing so, you have lost your total concentration on correctness and you are holding the gun up longer than you should, all the time using up energy needed for the rest of the match. Dressing up shots will more often cost you more points than it will get you. When you realize that you are doing it, you will also realize that you are UNCOMFORTABLE. Stop being UNCOMFORTABLE.

A finely tuned gun may have no perceived "creep" at all in the trigger. Creep is any movement of the trigger before hammer fall, and no matter how finely tuned a gun is, it does have creep. When you are letting out that last breath, or half breath, learn to judge the amount of finger pressure needed to create hammer-fall. It will take time and patience to acquire a good shooter's finger. The cheapest way to do this is to do a lot of dry firing which is good for you anyway. Knowing how to take up that creep is essential for getting that first shot to break as the targets start to turn or as the command/signal to fire is given.

Practice can be done with an empty gun in your house or at the range with live ammunition. The first option may be the most convenient and the easiest, but whichever, what you do and how you do it, will carry over to the competitive firing line. By that I mean some of the mechanics and all of the principles.

One good type of practice is called, "dry firing." This involves no ammunition, but squeezing the trigger until the hammer falls on an empty chamber. With some firearms this is not recommended. Some recommend inserting a commercially produced "Snap-Cap" dummy cartridge or an empty case in the chamber first. With some semi-automatic pistols it can be done without the empty case, although I would recommend using one anyway. The dummy rounds have no primers or powder in them and their purpose is to prevent damage to the firing pin. Dry firing is also an excellent way to perfect your line skills and it's a whole lot cheaper than shooting live ammunition.

During your practice sessions, you should strive to be aware of the sight picture as it last appeared to you when the hammer fell, i.e. in dry fire practice, without a target, what was the relationship of the front sight to the rear sight at the instant the hammer fell? In dry fire with a dot on the wall, or live fire practice with a target, the relationship is front sight to rear sight, and then that relationship relative to the target. If your sight picture is sharp, and your concentration is on the top of the front sight, you'll eventually be able to "call" every shot and be able to tell where that shot would have struck the target, and with surprising accuracy. When the hammer falls, quickly shut your eyes and concentrate on the last sight picture you saw when the hammer fell. By thinking of the target as a clock face, in a relatively short time, you should be able to say with a high degree of certainty where that shot hit—at eleven o'clock in the seven ring, or three o'clock in the nine ring, etc.

A tool that you may find very useful in your practice sessions at the range involves the use of some of those dummy rounds for center fire guns. Pick up five rounds, one of which is the dummy round, and without watching, load the clip or the cylinder with the five rounds. You should not know where the dummy round is in the loading process. Place it randomly so that you have no way of knowing when it will be the round in the chamber. If you have any tendency at all to jerk the trigger instead of squeezing it, this little trick will make it very evident to you. If the front sight takes a dive or a jump up just as, or before, the hammer falls on a dummy round you'll know you still have some work to do on trigger control and concentration.

This next entry I'm going to attach to the practice section, but its importance is as relevant in the ATTITUDE section as it is here. These two sections are so intertwined and inseparable that they really belong under a single heading.

If you are going to the range to practice under conditions as close to match conditions as you can get, and are going to actually be firing your gun, keep the following point in mind. Just because you brought along one box of fifty rounds, or a brick of 500 rounds, doesn't mean that you have to shoot all of them, or even a lot of them. Practice only what you know is right repeatedly. Get the physical positioning and other positive qualities as firmly engrained in your psyche, your brain and your body's muscle memory, as you can, and then transform those positive qualities from memories to automatic conditioned responses for when you step up to the firing line for a score.

That's the enjoyable and good part of practicing. On those days you smile a lot and feel like you've accomplished something and you have a right to be happy. However, on the down side, which happens more often, is your inability to recognize the reasons why things aren't going right and no matter what you do, they don't get any better. Most often, it will be a mental thing that gets in your way. Something just doesn't feel quite right. There's a lurking bit of uncertainty and a mild, seemingly uncorrectable, nagging DISCOMFORT about what you're trying to do.

At such times, if there's no one with you in an instructor's role, stop shooting, put the gear away and go home. The danger, if you want to call it that, is if you continue to shoot, you will simply reinforce unworkable conditions that you already know are wrong but for some reason aren't recognizing and can't identify. There are days like that, sometimes a lot of them, even for the best shooters when it simply just isn't working and no amount of trying will make it happen correctly. Firing a lot of rounds when things are not working so you can justify the time spent and the trip to the range is not using your head and it's really counterproductive. Accept it as part of your shooting evolution. Be philosophical about it, pack it up and go home. There will be better tomorrows.

If your attitude is upbeat and positive and you're committed to improving yourself and don't like unanswered questions, you will realize that your practice sessions are not entirely over just because you packed the guns away for the day and left the range. Now is the time to mentally regurgitate and review everything positive that you learned or was taught to you. Step by small step, phrase by phrase, item by small item and image by image, run and rerun those teachings through your mind like a film loop, again and again. Then rerun your last practice session through your mind, every little fragment and segment of it—good, bad, or indifferent—exactly the same way and compare the teachings to the practice session. You may be surprised when you find that some aspects don't match. Dwell on the differences when you find them. Then run the correct images from preparation to hammer-fall through your mind several times again. You'll be better for it.

Knowing why you do well is more important than knowing why you perform at less than your ability or not well. It gives you something which is positive to hang on to, to build on and to grow and mature with. The pluses have been, and always will be, better teachers than the negatives. A good shooter knows that he's good, but he also knows where his weak points are and works hard to minimize them. The negatives should be on a list that gets shorter and shorter as you practice to eliminate them. To perform as a champion, your practice sessions must evolve into, and take on the qualities of championship techniques, mechanical and mental.

Under the PRACTICE heading, I'm going to include a few tips about timed and rapid-fire shooting.

Obviously, in timed fire, which allows you twenty seconds to fire five shots, you're not going to put the gun down after six seconds as is recommended in slow fire. In both the timed and rapid-fire stages if you get the first shot to break at the precise moment you get the signal to shoot, you still have the original twenty, or ten, seconds for the remaining four shots of that string. In the timed fire stage, I usually take a breath after the second and fourth shots. Some shooters hold their breath for the full twenty seconds plus. Others shoot the timed stage as if it were rapid fire and fire the five-shot string in ten seconds. That's not a practice that I would recommend. In rapid-fire I take only the initial moderate breaths and then let it all out, just as in each shot of slow fire. The theory behind the firing of the timed fire stage in ten seconds rather than twenty seconds does have some merit attached to it. Let me assure you that there are major benefits to having that "extra" time to fire the five shots. For some, quicker is not always better, especially in shooting.

In what is known as a 2700 match, or a three-gun match—.22, center fire, and .45—some shooters carry only two guns, a .22 and a .45. The reasoning is, that since the .45 is a center fire gun, and they have to shoot the .45 anyway, just become proficient with the .45, shoot it twice and dispense with a third caliber center fire gun. The cost of the third gun and different ammunition is gone. The time needed to practice with a third gun is gone. In addition, if you reload your own ammunition, the time needed for reloading is also gone.

Practice what works for you, not what doesn't. Whatever you come up with, don't continue to shoot if you're aware that you need to take a breath. If you do continue without taking a needed breath you've just lost your concentration on the front sight. Take a breath sufficient to allow you to continue. The depth and the frequency of your pattern of breathing will be something you'll need to work out in your practice sessions.

The six-second time frame referred to in slow fire, is of necessity, stretched a little in the rapid-fire stage. If you have sufficient oxygen in your system and you're concentrating on the sight, you shouldn't even be aware that you've held your breath, or need to breathe, for ten or twelve, or even fifteen seconds.

In both timed and rapid-fire stages it's good conservation of time and to your advantage to get that first shot to break at the precise instant you see or hear the command to fire. Practice bringing the gun up, your breathing repetitions and getting your sights aligned, all at the same time, and still have sufficient time left to feel unhurried and COMFORTABLE about the coming series of shots.

Ideally, you should achieve your perfect sight picture at the exact moment you start to hold your breath, or as I do, let my breath out, and that should occur one to three seconds before the command to fire is given.

To prepare yourself for the three different stages of fire, you must be familiar with the commands that direct you to be, or ask you if you are, ready to fire the next string of shots. In all NRA sanctioned shoulder-to-shoulder 2700 pistol matches the commands are the same. The commands are given at about three-second intervals and are as follows:

"SHOOTERS ON THE LINE, THIS IS THE FIRST/SECOND STAGE OF THE SLOW-FIRE PORTION OF THE MATCH, WITH TEN SHOTS IN TEN MINUTES."

"WITH FIVE ROUNDS, LOAD! . . . LOAD YOUR SECOND FIVE ROUNDS WITHOUT COMMAND."

You will hear that sequence of commands at least twice in each match for each gun, once for each slow-fire target (ten shots). Then, three seconds later . . .

"IS THE LINE READY?"

Some shooters think this question is simply verbiage that the official caller of the match is required to say to conduct the match. It is not. A responsible caller is in charge of the range and is looking up and down the line of shooters at all times. He's looking for conditions that signal trouble and/or indicate that the match should be momentarily delayed or stopped, either for safety reasons or for the shooters benefit. He genuinely wants to know if you're not ready, and he wants you to say so if you're not. Since it is a question, and it's directed at you the shooter, if you're not ready to proceed, say so, loudly, "NOT READY," and raise your hand high. Wave your hand if need be. If a line officer sees that you are not ready he will hold up his paddle for the match caller to see. When the match caller sees that paddle being waved, he will call out, "THE LINE IS NOT READY. SHOOTERS STAND AT EASE."

A line officer will/should then come to you to check out the reason for you calling "Not Ready" and raising your hand, and possibly offer assistance to get you ready quickly. If it looks like your problem is going to take some time to correct he may simply tell you to make the gun safe, bench it and step back from the line so the match can continue with a high degree of continuity. Do not argue with him and do not worry about it. Your concerns will be addressed after that string of fire and you will be allowed to shoot all your shots if your reasons for not being ready are deemed justifiable according to the rules.

In the event that you are not heard or seen and the match continues despite your problems and your gesturing, don't get excited. Just remove the clip, lay your gun on the bench, make the gun as safe as you can or put it in your shooting box, step away from the line and wait until that string of fire is over, whether it's ten minutes, twenty or ten seconds. That string of fire will continue without you.

Do not try to fix your problem and do not disturb the other shooters. Stand quietly until the caller declares a cease-fire and the shooting period has expired. If you have a legitimate reason for not being ready you'll be given an equal chance to fire your shots in what's called an "Alibi string." Productive practices, regular equipment maintenance, and detailed checklist preparations will pretty much eliminate your need to yell, "Not Ready."

If someone else is recognized as not ready, simply lower your pistol to the bench, maintaining your position grip with relaxed gripping pressure, and wait. Whether their problem is fixed in a hurry or not, when the line official's paddles go down and the line officers indicate that the match should continue, the match caller will (may) say, "THE COMMAND TO LOAD HAS BEEN GIVEN." About three seconds later, and at subsequent three-second intervals the following calls become statements, as was the last command, and not questions . . .

"THE LINE IS READY." Once this command is given, the match will proceed unless an unsafe condition has been discovered.

"READY ON THE LEFT."
"READY ON THE RIGHT."
"READY ON THE FIRING LINE!"
"FIRE!"

The command to "FIRE" can be given, or made unmistakably evident in a variety of ways. You may hear the word "Fire" called out loudly, or you may see the targets turn 90 degrees, or hear a referee-type whistle, or hear an electric buzzer, or see a light for deaf shooters or whatever signal is used at that range.

However, if a range is equipped with turning targets there will be no spoken or illuminated command to fire or to cease firing. If it is the slow-fire stage of the match the caller will (may) call out, "YOU HAVE TEN MINUTES."

The time-fire and rapid-fire stages of the match will be called as follows:

"THIS IS THE 1ST/2ND STAGE OF THE TIME/RAPID FIRE PORTION OF THE MATCH WITH TWO FIVE-SHOT STRINGS IN 20/10 SECONDS. ON THE LINE, WITH FIVE ROUNDS, LOAD."

Except for NOT loading and firing the second series of five shots, until directed to do so, the commands and the timing of the commands are the same as the slow-fire portion of the match.

Until the command to load has been given, do not insert your next clip into your gun. For all intents and purposes, and legally, that is a loaded gun. Not only can it be dangerous but also it gains you nothing. Get used to shooting safely.

After each string of five shots in timed and rapid-fire, the caller will ask the line, "Are there any alibis?" He's asking if there are any shooters that were unable to shoot all five rounds for reasons other than what are considered the shooter's fault. After a line officer checks the situation, and the reasons are determined to be legitimate, any shooters with legitimate alibis will be given an opportunity to shoot an alibi string of five shots on the same target. An alibi target may end up having fourteen holes in it, of which only the low ten hits are scored. If your alibi request is disallowed you will only get credit for the bullet holes presently in the target and you will not be allowed to fire an alibi string.

Each practice session and each match you attend may have different people "calling" the event. Generally speaking, whatever their rhythm and the decibel level of the commands, they are usually pretty consistent throughout the match. Whether you like the way they are doing it or not, adjust to it as quickly as you can and use it to your benefit. If there is a variance from the "about three seconds" timing, it is usually to be faster. Don't dwell on such meaningless details that can invade your concentration.

The time-frame from the time you start your breathing preparations to the time your sights are perfectly aligned on the target and you are ready to start your squeeze on the trigger should become a workable constant for you. It's what you will do. every time commands are given to the line. Practice being ready to shoot approximately two seconds before the command to fire is given. While you are going through your routine, listen intently to the caller's timing for each command. If the signal to fire is a called command and you are having trouble hearing the commands, you may not be expecting the "fire" command and be startled when others start to fire their guns. If that should happen, your concentration will also be late, quite possibly never regained or catching up with the time allowed. Ask the caller to please call louder.

I mentioned it before but it's worth restating. To get that first shot to break at that precise moment when the "signal" of fire is given is significantly important. If that first shot breaks when it should, you have just given yourself a twenty percent time gift to get the job done, a very important twenty percent. Take advantage of it. It's another plus for you.

DO NOT hurry your shots in any stage of a match. Hurry produces bad shots, that produce low scores, that produce unhappy shooters, that now struggle to produce even more not-so-good shots. It's better to have only four good shots in a string than five bad shots.

Sometime during your many practice sessions with live ammo, adjust your sight three or four clicks to the left or right just to see what that translates to at the target. Don't be afraid to make adjustments to your sights. You can be just as wrong on the other side of the 10 or X and still get the same score. You should already know or have ready access to this information before you step to the line in competition. There is literature available that gives adjusting data about every adjustable open sight on the market or that comes as standard equipment on guns.

Have your shots suddenly moved left or right? Check your grip first. If that is as it should be, check the sights to see if they're suddenly loose. If those items are as they should be, then adjust the sight. Remember, you are part of your equipment and you just may be the part that is failing to do its job. Think about it.

Throughout this writing, as I warned you, you have noticed the word COMFORT in capital letters wherever it appears. The reason for that is also worth repeating. It is because of the importance that word will play in any degree of success you will achieve as a shooter. Remember . . . if you are COMFORTABLE on the line, you will be more COMFORTABLE at the scoreboard after the match. COMFORT should come before you squeeze the trigger and remain your partner for the entire match.

To go along with that, another philosopher once said, "A really great talent finds its happiness in execution."

– Johann Wolfgang Von Goethe

Keep your eye on the front sight, and may all your shots be COMFORTABLE 10s and Xs.

– Garet L. Garrett, 2012

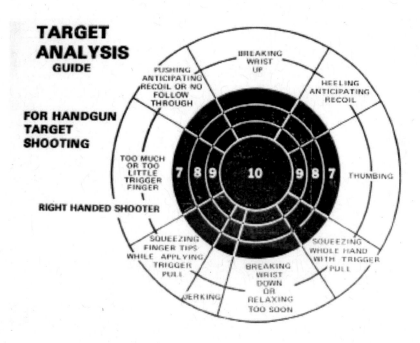

TARGET ANALYSIS GUIDE

FOR HANDGUN TARGET SHOOTING

RIGHT HANDED SHOOTER

BREAKING WRIST UP

PUSHING ANTICIPATING RECOIL OR NO FOLLOW THROUGH

HEELING ANTICIPATING RECOIL

TOO MUCH OR TOO LITTLE TRIGGER FINGER

THUMBING

SQUEEZING FINGER TIPS WHILE APPLYING TRIGGER PULL

JERKING

BREAKING WRIST DOWN OR RELAXING TOO SOON

SQUEEZING WHOLE HAND WITH TRIGGER PULL

7 8 9 10 9 8 7

About the Author
Garet L. Garrett

I started shooting skeet when I was ten years old with my father and two brothers at the Emmet County Sportsman's Club in Petoskey, Michigan in 1947. I was a trap-house boy for many years back then, since our traps required pull wires and muscle power. For pulling the trip levers and loading the traps my father awarded me the privilege of shooting a round of skeet each Sunday. As I got older, and my third brother joined us, I became more than capable of holding my own with any of the "old timers."

Right out of high school I served six years active in the Air Force. Fourteen years later I joined a Naval reserves CB detachment for two years, and then followed that up in 1980 with eight years in the Army's IRR program attached to the 5077th SMU, 123rd ARCOM, 5th Army. It was while I was in the Army reserves marksmanship unit that I got some "serious" lessons in pistol and rifle shooting from experts.

My introduction to competitive shooting started in 1975 when I was invited by a co-worker, Sfc. Rolf V. Henretty, to participate in a winter league shooting .22 pistols. Since I had grown up with guns and enjoyed shooting, that first league session was enough to hook me for life.

I subsequently made five trips to Camp Perry, Ohio, to participate in the National Pistol Championship Matches and I view those trips as some of the most enjoyable shooting moments of my life. The people that I traveled to the matches with had a lot to do with that.

Over the years I have competed in skeet, trap, "2700" pistol competitions, four position and prone .22 rifle competitions, high power rifle competitions, both militarily and as a civilian, and am presently involved in schuetzen competition. All of these disciplines of shooting have been a great joy to me, largely because of the people I have met and the friends I have made over the years through participation in shooting events.